The Government and Politics of the Alberta Metis Settlements

The Government and Politics of the Alberta Metis Settlements

T.C. Pocklington

Canadian Plains Research Center
University of Regina
1991

Copyright © Canadian Plains Research Center

Copyright Notice

All rights reserved. No part of this book covered by the copyrights hereon may be reproduced or used in any form or by any means—graphic, electronic or mechanical—without the prior written permission of the publisher. Any request for photocopying, recording, taping or information storage and retrieval systems of any part of this book shall be directed in writing to the Canadian Reprography Collective, 379 Adelaide Street West, Suite M1, Toronto, Ontario M5V 1S5.

Canadian Plains Research Center
University of Regina
Regina, Saskatchewan S4S 0A2
Canada

∞
Printed on acid-free paper

Canadian Cataloguing in Publication Data

Pocklington, T.C. (Thomas C.)
The government and politics of Alberta Metis Settlements

1st ed. —

(Canadian plains studies, ISSN 0317-6290 ; 20)
Includes bibliographical references.
ISBN 0-88977-060-3

1. Metis - Alberta - Politics and government.
2. Metis - Alberta - Government relations. 3. Metis
- Alberta - Land tenure. 4. Metis - Alberta -
Social conditions. I. University of Regina.
Canadian Plains Research Center. II. Title.
III. Series.

FC126.A4P62 1991   323.1'197'07123   C90-097029-4
E99.M693P62 1991

Cover Design: Brian Mlazgar
Printed and bound in Canada by
Friesen Printers, Altona, Manitoba

Dedication

For Lou

CONTENTS

Tables	viii
Preface	ix
Introduction	xiii
1. Prelude to the Formation of the Alberta Metis Settlements	1
2. Legal Status of the Alberta Metis Settlements	24
3. Government and Politics of the Metis Settlements: An Overview	35
4. Councillors of the Metis Settlements	45
5. The Alberta Federation of Metis Settlement Associations	61
6. The Metis Development Branch	73
7. External Political Orientations of the Metis Settlers	88
8. Internal Political Orientations of the Metis Settlers	103
9. The Self-Government Issue	123
10. Conferences and Negotiations	137
Epilogue	153
Selected Bibliography	156
Index	159

TABLES

1. Age of Metis Settlement Councillors, 1984	46
2. Formal Education of Metis Settlement Councillors, 1984	47
3. Party Voting of Councillors, 1980 Federal Election	50
4. Party Voting of Councillors, 1982 Provincial Election	52
5. Greatest Perceived Problem of Settlement, 1984	56
6. Second-Greatest Perceived Problem of Settlement, 1984	57
7. Councillors' Positions on Greater Political Independence for Settlements, 1984	59
8. Helpfulness of FMSA to Metis Settlements	70
9. Performance of FMSA President	70
10. Vote Budget, 1984-1985	77
11. Trust Budget, 1984-1985	78
12. Budget of the FMSA, 1984-1985	78
13. Age Distribution of Respondents	91
14. Leading Families: Interviewed and Actual	92
15. Formal Education of Respondents	93
16. Competence in Cree of Respondents	93
17. Religious Affiliations of Respondents	94
18. Duration of Residence	95
19. Professed Voting of Respondents, 1980 Federal Election	96
20. Professed Voting of Respondents, 1982 Provincial Election	98
21. Membership in the MAA	101
22. Performance of Settlement Council	107
23. Responsiveness of Settlement Council	108
24. Opinions About Self-Government	111
25. Perceived Favouritism	115

PREFACE

In 1978 I was invited to devise and teach an intensive introductory university-level course in political science at the Blue Quills Native Education Centre near St. Paul, Alberta. The course I taught was labelled "Political Action: Strategy, Tactics, and Morality in a Liberal Democracy." In its emphasis on effective and defensible means to ends, I think the course was on the right track. However, I felt that, from the standpoint of the students, it was far less rewarding than it should have been.

The principal defect of the course was that I was unable sufficiently to employ my greatest strength as a teacher—relating theoretical considerations to the concrete experiences of the students. Part of the problem was that I had next to no personal experience of life on an Indian reserve or in a Metis community, let alone real familiarity with the substance and roots of political cooperation and conflict within such collectivities. The other, and more galling, part of the problem was that I could find almost no literature to help reduce my ignorance. Historians, anthropologists and, increasingly, lawyers were making valuable contributions to Native studies, but political scientists were not holding up their end. I could find nothing that presented sustained description, analysis or prescription regarding the current state of government and politics in a Native community. To the extent that *anyone* was writing about current Native politics, the focus was almost exclusively on provincial, territorial and national Indian organizations and prominent figures within them: too many chiefs and no Indians (even here the Metis were "the forgotten people"). The only books that came remotely close to meeting the needs of me and my students were Harold Cardinal's two powerful indictments, *The Unjust Society* (Edmonton: Hurtig, 1969) and *The Rebirth of Canada's Indians* (Edmonton: Hurtig, 1977), which however have more the character of manifestoes than inquiries, and Edgar Dosman's admirable, pathbreaking *Indians: The Urban Dilemma* (Toronto: McClelland and Stewart, 1972), which is only marginally relevant to Native people living in rural areas. I think it was at this time that the idea of writing something about Native politics at the community level first occurred to me.

The result of my ignorance and the lack of suitable literature to mitigate it was that the course was transformed. In brief, I taught the students an introductory course in Canadian politics and political theory while they taught me an introductory course in Native politics. The contributions of the students were invaluable, but flawed. First, their observations were invariably anecdotal. Second, as several students told me in private conversation once I had gained their trust, on a number of matters students were suppressing or distorting information and concealing or muting their views. In face-to-face societies, they told me, especially those in which family and clan loyalties are extraordinarily important, public airing of certain facts and opinions could be disruptive of social harmony and disadvantageous to the incautious speaker. Having been shown (albeit very courteously) my ignorance and naivety about Native society and politics, I was resolved to learn more.

My experience at Blue Quills was not formative only because it was in some respects humiliating. As a resident at the school, along with a number of secondary and postsecondary students, I received—at first reluctantly but then more and more enthusiastically—an immersion course in aspects of the beliefs, experiences, social conditions, hopes and fears of some of the Plains Cree of east-central Alberta. In addition to innumerable "bull sessions," I was invited to social gatherings at the nearest reserve and was exposed to the teachings of some of the elders. Increasingly I became fascinated with Native ways of life, particularly (and not surprisingly in light of my background) with the politics of Native communities.

After I left Blue Quills my interest in Native life, especially political life, intensified rather than waned. I began to read more and more extensively, did some research work for a small Native political organization in exchange for instruction in the Cree language, and became active in the efforts to establish a School of Native Studies at the University of Alberta. These experiences strengthened my conviction that there was a real need for a searching examination of the government and politics of a Native community.

Around this time, I remade the acquaintance of an old friend who was then the president of the Alberta Federation of Metis Settlement Associations (FMSA). I did not know at the time that he held this position. For that matter, the little I knew about the Metis settlements consisted of vague recollections of sections of books and articles on broader topics. Under his tutelage my ignorance of the settlements gradually declined, to be replaced by fascination. Before long, the settlements seemed to me the ideal site for the kind of study I had in mind. I broached the idea to my friend. He was enthusiastic, especially because I proposed to spend time on the settlements talking to ordinary folks instead of confining myself to library research and discussions with Metis leaders and government officials. However, he emphasized that it was not within his power to give or withhold consent. Authorization would have to be given both by the board of directors of the FMSA and by the council (and perhaps also a general meeting) of any settlement in which I proposed to conduct interviews. I prepared an outline of the study I proposed to conduct, and eventually received permission from the FMSA board and two settlements to undertake the project.

Although it is somewhat lengthy and aims at a certain thoroughness, in that it does not confine its attention to the internal politics of the settlements and the FMSA but also examines their relationships with external public and private agencies, it cannot be emphasized too strongly that this study is exploratory in character. Partly because I had no model to emulate, this exploration raises more questions than it answers. I hope that readers learn something from the following pages, but I hope more fervently that subsequent researchers (including Metis and other Native communities that choose to study themselves) will find here an inquiry that is worth improving upon.

This study is addressed to several audiences. First in my heart are the Metis settlers and their political leaders. No doubt they will find in these pages some comments that are so obvious as to be not worth mentioning, and others that are so far off base as to be undeserving of rebuttal. But I will be surprised as well as disappointed if they do not discover here some insights into their political institutions and practices. If they do find something of value here, that will be merely partial repayment of a debt, since they brought to my attention some of the peculiarities of my own Euro-Canadian preconceptions.

Second, I have not forgotten my students at Blue Quills. I hope this book will help to fill a gap in their political education and that of their children. More generally, I hope it will be found useful by university and college students in Native Studies programs, as well as in political science courses (especially in Canadian government, public policy and comparative politics), which generally pay far too little attention to Native government and politics.

Finally, this inquiry is addressed to two audiences often, but I believe wrongly, thought to be mutually exclusive—scholars who specialize in the study of Native peoples and general readers interested in Native political circumstances, problems, aspirations and progress. While neither the substance nor the style of this book is calculated to put it on the shelf of the airport gift shop, I try to meet reasonable standards of scholarship in language that is straightforward and free of unnecessary jargon.

In the course of writing this book I incurred debts to a number of people, the most important of whom must remain anonymous. The settlers I interviewed in the communities disguised here with the names "Osprey Lake" and "Paskwaw" were extremely patient, forthcoming and hospitable. So, too, were the councillors of these (as well as the other six) settlements, and the directors and executive officers of the FMSA. I wish to thank especially the leaders and staff members of the FMSA who read and commented on all or part of the manuscript. Members of the Metis Development Branch (MDB) of the Alberta Department of Municipal Affairs were also generous with their time, both in Edmonton and in the field. So, too, were several members of the staff of the Native Secretariat.

As to people I can name, Michael Asch provided me with advice and bits of useful information and leads as to where to find more. My long-standing closest associates, Don Carmichael and Greg Pyrcz, put through their paces my views on Native self-government. Leah Modin typed successive drafts of the manuscript with her usual speed, accuracy and tolerance. Copy editing and proofreading were done by Brian Mlazgar and Agnes Bray, of the Canadian Plains Research Center, University of Regina. I wish to thank the University of Alberta for providing me with a grant to help offset the cost of travel and sustenance while visiting the settlements and later a course reduction to permit sustained work on the manuscript.

INTRODUCTION

In northern Alberta there are eight Metis settlements, which have a combined area of 1.25 million acres. This is the only collective Metis land base in Canada. The Alberta Metis settlements (originally, and still occasionally, referred to as colonies) were established in the last years of the Great Depression. They were intended mainly as a welfare scheme that would help relieve the most destitute Metis without further large welfare expenditures. From the beginning, it was specified in law that the Metis settlers should be represented on the board that provided the local government for each settlement. In fact, however, a local manager—a civil servant employed by the provincial government—initially made all decisions of any consequence.

During the past five decades there have been changes in almost every aspect of life on the settlements. As its title suggests, this book concentrates on settlement government and politics. On first consideration, this focus may seem to be very limited, but unless one's conceptions of government and politics are indefensibly narrow, an attempt to understand them even as they function in small communities like the settlements is intimidating. In the first place, the *range* of relationships that must be examined is daunting. Settlement political life is an amalgam of the relationships among "ordinary" residents of the settlements, settlement politicians (considered both as individuals and as members of the settlement council, as the settlement governing bodies are now known), the FMSA (the settlements' coordinating and lobbying agency), provincial and federal politicians and civil servants, and an array of pressure groups—Native and non-Native, provincial, regional and national. It is difficult to identify the various players, much less to discover how they interact.

An attempt to understand the government and politics of the settlements is also intimidating because there is no single key to comprehension. There is no general political theory to bring coherence to one's investigations. Nor can coherence be imposed usefully by concentrating on a particular theme or issue. Of course it would be *possible* to confine attention to a theme like the role of family loyalties in settlement politics, or to an issue like "self-government." But to do so would purchase neatness at the price of ignoring the richness of Metis politics. Finally, it makes no sense to rely on a single type or method of inquiry. The study of settlement government and politics requires the use of standard tools employed by political scientists for the description and analysis of political institutions and practices, but in various of its phases the study must also rely on interviews and on historical, legal and philosophical analysis and speculation.

Of necessity, this book undertakes to explore a terrain rather than answer a question. It begins by recounting some of the main historical events, especially the proximate events, that led to the formation of the Alberta Metis settlements. Chapter 2 deals with the legal status of the settlements: their powers and responsibilities, liabilities and limitations. It is a mistake to underestimate the influence of law on the structure and functioning of governmental institutions and political practices. At the very least, law imposes a framework on political activity, inviting some lines of action and discouraging others.

However, it is also a mistake to overestimate the political import of law. It is impossible for law to be comprehensive enough to regulate all political activity. Even when law clearly does apply, it is supplemented (and sometimes altered or even undermined) by informal codes of conduct that guide political behaviour. Thus, a sound grasp of political reality must probe beyond the provisions of law. In Chapter 3 we begin to examine the government and politics of the settlements from a perspective that takes account of extralegal political realities. The purpose of this chapter is to provide a broad overview of the organizations and officials, and their interrelationships, that influence the patterns of government and politics on the settlements. Although it goes beyond legalities to political realities, this chapter is still much more descriptive than analytical: it provides a sketch of institutions and interrelationships without making an effort to see how they operate.

The next three chapters involve more intensive analysis. Each examines one of the three elite groups that have the largest impact on settlement government. Chapter 4 examines the composition, organization and activities of the local governments of the settlements, the settlement councils. Chapter 5 performs the same task for the settlements' coordinating and lobbying agency, the Alberta FMSA. Chapter 6 examines the structure and functioning of the government agency with which the settlement councils and the FMSA have had the most frequent dealings, the MDB of the Alberta Department of Municipal Affairs.

Chapters 7 and 8 deal with an important factor that is typically ignored in studies of Native politics. As a rule, studies of Native politics concentrate exclusively on regionally and nationally prominent organizations and individuals. These chapters, which are based on extensive interviews conducted on two of the settlements, attempt to reveal something of the political attitudes, opinions and activities of "rank-and-file" settlers, including their assessments of their leaders.

Chapter 9 addresses the issue that currently preoccupies many Natives and commentators on Native law and politics, the issue of self-government. This chapter argues for a philosophically more cogent approach to issues concerning Native political self-determination than is found in the usual doctrinaire statements commending or denouncing it. This approach is then applied tentatively to the situation of the Alberta Metis settlements. Chapter 10 is an attempt to provide a reasonably clear and concise description of the complex discussions and negotiations that have taken place, mainly in the last five years, between Metis and government officials concerning the main issues that continue to divide them.

1

Prelude to the Formation of the Alberta Metis Settlements

There is a view of Metis history which, though it has long been rejected by scholars, can fairly be described as the conventional view. The most prominent feature of this view is that the story of the Metis is a colourful *episode* in Canadian history, an episode essentially limited to the period between the Red River uprising of 1870 and the North-West Rebellion of 1885. This portrait of the Metis has several noteworthy features. Geographically, the focus is almost entirely on the Red River Settlement and the southern Saskatchewan communities which were the site of the 1885 uprising. Demographically, although the Scottish Selkirk Settlers and their Metis progeny are not completely ignored, the Metis are construed as overwhelmingly French and Catholic.[1] Mixed-bloods of British or other non-French ancestry are taken to be peripheral not only in numbers but also in enthusiasm for the aspirations and activities of their French and Catholic cousins. Economically, the Metis are portrayed as dependent primarily on the buffalo hunt. The main basis of their economic life is taken to be provision of pemmican for the fur traders. This dependence on the buffalo is closely connected to a nomadism largely inconsistent with the economic activities, especially agriculture, which demand settled communities. Culturally, the Metis are regarded as having much more in common with their maternal than their paternal ancestors. Though nominally Christian, they are portrayed as fundamentally uncivilized, lacking in foresight, and living from day to day. Politically, the Metis are regarded as extraordinarily naive.

Thus, in its political dimension, the conventional account of the Metis concentrates almost exclusively on the person of Louis Riel. Riel is seen as unique in his educational accomplishments, oratorical skills (in French, English and Cree), organizing ability and comprehension of the practices of the British, Canadian and American governments. So pivotal is the political role assigned to Riel in this view that it would be no exaggeration to summarize it as follows: "no Riel, no rebellion."

The final ingredient in this version of Metis history is that it ended, and *had* to end, soon after the Rebellion of 1885. The Metis were essentially a primitive people who could not withstand the onslaught of the superior civilization brought by the white settlers who were flooding the Prairies. After their defeat in 1885, the Metis were doomed to be assimilated either into Euro-Canadian or Indian society, or else to live a marginal life on the fringes of one or the other. As a distinct people, the Metis died in 1885, but their death had been foreseeable and inescapable. George F.G. Stanley put it this way:

> The rebellion of 1885 was the last effort of the primitive peoples in Canada to withstand the inexorable advance of white civilization. With the suppression of the rebellion white dominance was assured. Henceforth the history of the Canadian West was to be that of the white man, not that of the red man or the bois brulé.[2]

What follows is not an attempt to provide even a capsule version of the real history of the Metis. Indeed, any attempt to produce a reliable summary would be foolhardy, since specialists in Metis history are daily casting doubt on generalizations that had been thought to be firmly established.[3] However, the conventional version of Metis history retains a strong hold, and it contains errors which could easily lead to misunderstandings of the current government and politics of the Metis settlements. An attempt to combat some of the misconceptions about Metis history is therefore highly pertinent to our subject.[4]

To begin with, the view that Metis history is nothing more than a brief episode in Canadian history, enclosed chronologically within two political/military uprisings, and geographically within the Red River and South Saskatchewan River valleys, is without foundation. As to the earlier temporal and geographical extreme, more than one commentator has remarked that the first person of mixed Indian and non-Indian ancestry was born approximately nine months after the first non-Indians arrived in North America. Summarizing a lengthy historical period, Jacqueline Peterson says that

> by 1815, tangible evidence of a 150-year-long alliance between men of the fur trade and native women was everywhere in abundance. Throughout the upper Great Lakes region, towns and villages populated by a people of mixed heritage illustrated the vitality of the intermarriage compact.[5]

However, prior to 1870 the presence of people of mixed heritage was not confined to the area from the Red River eastwards. Children of the fur trade, the Metis were found in fur trade posts as far west as the foothills of the Rocky Mountains in the late eighteenth and early nineteenth centuries. Thus, "by 1810 the Metis were firmly established across the West and South into what was to become United States' territory. Wherever buffalo or furs were to be found, there also were the Metis."[6]

Just as the mid-1800s is too late a date for the birth of the Metis, so reports of their demise shortly after 1885 have proven premature. In the western provinces and in the territories many people, both rural and urban, identify themselves as Metis, as is suggested by the vitality in these places of Metis political organizations.[7] The discussion of the Alberta Metis settlements in the following pages underlines the point that the Metis are still very much alive. Moreover, it is arguable that Metis communities have evolved in the recent past and that more may arise in the future. Thus, for example, the "mixed-bloods" of Grande Cache, a town in the high foothills northeast of Jasper, Alberta have decided during the past two decades to designate themselves as Metis.[8]

The official 1871 census of the Red River Colony stated that there were in the area 5,720 French-speaking Metis, 4,080 English-speaking Metis, and 1,600 whites.[9] Although there were more French than English-speaking Metis, it is simply not the case that the Metis were—or are—overwhelmingly French in descent and Catholic in faith. Nor is it the case that at Red River, or in southern Saskatchewan or further west, there were sharp cleavages amongst the Metis between French-speaking Catholics and English-speaking Protestants. The lifestyle of the two groups was essentially similar and intermarriage was common.[10] Present-day Metis have not been left a legacy of deep strife between Catholics of French heritage and Protestants of British descent.

The notion that the economy of the Metis at Red River and further west was dominated by the buffalo hunt, and that they were therefore predominantly nomadic, is likewise ill-founded. According to Duke Redbird, "not more than one-third of the Metis assembled for the fall hunt."[11] Whether or not Redbird's estimate is accurate, even those who did engage in the buffalo hunt did not follow it as a full-time occupation. Characteristically, buffalo hunters also ran small farms with large gardens, small plots of grain and a few head of livestock. Often, the income from these activities was supplemented by payment for casual work with the Hudson's Bay Company (HBC). Other Metis were permanent employees of the HBC, some of them attaining quite highly paid positions, but the majority working as clerks, canoemen, freighters and interpreters. They had permanent homes close to trading posts. Only a small proportion of the nineteenth-century Metis lived a life based almost exclusively on hunting and trapping, and therefore plausibly described as nomadic. The idea that the Metis generally were unsuited to a settled life does not bear scrutiny. Nor does the idea that they were generally uncivilized and lacking in foresight. Indeed, it is exceedingly difficult to reconcile this depiction of the Metis with the two events with which they are most commonly associated: the uprising of 1870 and the Rebellion of 1885. Explanations and evaluations of these two events differ widely, but none apparently denies that either of these campaigns of defiance was intended to protect what were deemed to be vital *long-term* interests of the Metis. Indeed, from at least as early as the Battle of Seven Oaks in 1816, the Metis demonstrated a continuing concern to establish and protect a land base and to exercise significant control over their own destiny. From the Battle of Seven Oaks, in which the Metis successfully challenged the HBC's declaration of a monopoly over the supply of pemmican, through the defeat by the Metis in 1849 of the HBC's prohibition of free trade in furs with the United States, the uprising in 1870 and the subsequent agreement by the government of Canada to the guarantee in the Manitoba Act of most of Metis demands, including both political rights and the reservation of 1.4 million acres of land for the Metis, the North-West Rebellion of 1885, in which further guarantees of land were solidified, to the present day, when land and political rights are being sought through litigation and political negotiation in various parts of Canada, the Metis have consistently sought a land base and a significant measure of self-determination *within* British North America and, later, Canada. It must be emphasized that the importance attached to land and political rights within the Alberta Metis settlements, which is discussed frequently in the following chapters, is by no means a break with earlier Metis history. On the contrary, it is but another step in a continuing tradition.

The preeminence given to Louis Riel in the nineteenth-century political history of the Metis—to the extent that we frequently hear of the "Riel Rebellions"—is unfortunate. The major concern is not that excessive attention to that extraordinary man oversimplifies complex events, although this may be the case. Nor is it that obsession with Riel distracts attention from the fact that there were other formidable Metis leaders in the period, such as Cuthbert Grant and Gabriel Dumont, although this may also be true. Even more important, at least from the standpoint of this study, is that inordinate concentration on the role of Riel tends to lend credence to the view that "rank-and-file" Metis were utterly unsophisticated politically. Neglected in the "Riel Rebellions" perspective is the fact that "ordinary" Metis were political forces to be reckoned with prior to and during both uprisings. For one example, consider that Riel was not a member of the tribunal which, in 1870, sentenced Thomas Scott to death, the "crime" for which Riel was eventually hanged. For another, consider that in the early 1880s (while Riel was living in the United States) the Metis of the Batoche-St. Laurent area formed their own governing council, which repeatedly petitioned the federal government for settlement of their land claims. It was this council that sent a delegation to Montana in 1884 to urge Riel to come and join their struggle. Of course, these remarks are not meant to suggest that Riel was not the major figure in nineteenth-century Metis politics. To recur to the two examples just mentioned, no doubt Riel could have prevented the execution of Scott, and no doubt the North-West Rebellion, if it had occurred at all, would have taken a quite different form without Riel's presence. The point is simply that the current political vitality of the Metis is not a birth but a rebirth. Metis political activism did not begin and end with Riel. Although they lay dormant for some years, the roots of Metis political energy and skill are deep and strong.

If one were to concentrate exclusively on the period between the suppression of the uprisings of 1870 and 1885, and the Great Depression of the 1930s, one could easily be persuaded by the conventional version of Metis history that 1885 marked the inevitable destruction of the primitive Metis by the advance of a superior white civilization. Pushed further and further west by the influx of European settlers, the drastic decline of the fur trade and the buffalo herds, the combination of short-sightedness and duplicity in the land policies of the Canadian government, and the distaste of some of them for a settled, agricultural style of life, descendents of the Red River Metis migrated after 1870 to all parts of the area that was to become Alberta, but especially to the central and northern regions, there to join Metis who had migrated to the area much earlier in the century.[12] A somewhat smaller, but still considerable, influx occurred after the defeat of 1885.[13]

By the 1860s both the fur trade and the buffalo herds were in decline. Indeed, by 1880 the last of the great buffalo herds had been slaughtered. In spite of their movement westward in retreat from white settlement and in search of open land, the condition of the Metis was becoming increasingly desperate. Some indication of the desperation of their condition at the end of the nineteenth century and in the first three decades of the twentieth century can be conveyed by a brief comparison of their circumstances with the abysmal but nevertheless better situation of their Indian cousins.[14]

Relative Situations of the Indians and the Metis

By far the most important difference between the Indians and the Metis is that the former acquired, at least legally, a secure land base while the latter did not. Between 1876 and 1899 treaties were negotiated which extinguished Indian aboriginal title to all but a small area of Alberta (which came under treaty not long after Alberta gained provincial status in 1905). In compensation, reserve land was granted to the Indian bands on the basis of one square mile per family of five persons. (Treaty 8 also permitted allocation on the basis of a different formula, the complexities of which need not detain us here.) In addition, band members received a one-time cash payment plus an annual cash payment to each band member in perpetuity. The treaties gave to the government the right to appropriate reserve lands for public purposes, with compensation. They also permitted the government to sell or lease reserve lands with the consent of the band in question, but they prohibited Indians from selling or leasing land on their own initiative. In addition, Indians retained the right to hunt, fish and trap on the unsettled land they surrendered, as well as on their reserve land.[15]

The Metis were treated quite differently from the Indians in regard to land. Although it was recognized that the Metis, too, had aboriginal land rights, the extinction of their rights was accomplished by unilateral action by the government rather than by negotiation and treaty. Moreover, Metis aboriginal land rights were extinguished on an individual rather than a collective basis. Certificates called "scrip," which entitled their possessors to a specified number of acres of Dominion land ("land scrip"), or to a cash value redeemable in the purchase of Dominion land ("money scrip"), were allotted to eligible recipients. The history of the allotment and distribution of scrip is too long and complex to examine in detail here, but the following may be taken as a typical pattern. Metis children born before a specified date were given the choice between a land scrip which they could redeem for 240 acres of Dominion land, or a money scrip valued at $240 with which they could purchase Dominion land. "Heads of households" were likewise given a choice between the two kinds of scrip, but their values were limited to 160 acres or $160. For a variety of reasons, the granting of scrip provided few benefits to the Metis. Most often the scrip passed quickly into the hands of land speculators. As a result, most of the Metis were left landless.[16] Moreover, unlike the Indians, the Metis were subject to laws of general application in regard to hunting, fishing and trapping.

Indian possession, and Metis lack, of a land base was the most important difference between the situations of the two groups. Most of the treaties specified that the bands were to be provided with various equipment—such as ammunition and agricultural implements—to enable them to make better use of their land. All the treaties required that a school was to be established on each reserve, and this has been interpreted subsequently to mean free tuition at all levels of education, although governments regularly attempt to abridge this right. Furthermore, Treaty 6 contained the provision that "a medicine chest shall be kept at the house of each Indian Agent for the use and benefit of the Indians, at the discretion of such Agent," which has been interpreted to mean free medical care for all Indians. Finally, section 91(24) of the Constitution Act gave the federal government legislative jurisdiction over "Indians, and Lands reserved for the Indians," thus assigning to the federal government responsibility for the well-being of Indians. Although the Indian Act specifically excludes "any person of the race of aborigines commonly referred to as Eskimos," the Supreme Court of Canada held that the Inuit were "Indians" within the meaning of section 91(24). But the provision excluding anyone who "has received or has been allotted half-breed lands or money scrip" remains intact.[17]

This comparison is not meant to suggest that the condition of the Indians was enviable or that they were treated magnanimously by the government of Canada; it is only meant to indicate that the condition of the Metis was far worse. At the end of the nineteenth century and in the early decades of the twentieth century, most of the Metis were living in scattered bands, landless, disease ridden, and without hope of pursuing their traditional manner of life. The circumstances of the Alberta Metis were especially grim in the central and north-central regions. The relatively few Metis who migrated into the southern part of the province tended to assimilate into the dominant society, and those in the north were able to pursue some semblance of their traditional lifestyle. But in the central regions game was scarce, prohibitively expensive fishing licences were required, and white settlement was spreading remorselessly. The majority of the Metis were reduced to squatting on the fringes of Indian reserves and white settlements and on road allowances.

St. Paul des Métis

In 1895 Father Albert Lacombe, who had a sincere, if paternalistic, concern for the Metis, approached the federal government with a proposal to establish a farming colony for the Metis, "A Philanthropic

Plan to Redeem the Half-breeds of Manitoba and the North-West Territories." This scheme, which established a precedent for the formation of the Metis settlements, promised advantages to both government and church, quite apart from humanitarian and spiritual considerations. From the standpoint of the government, a principal virtue of the plan was that it promised to be cheap—far less expensive than scrip. From the standpoint of the Roman Catholic Church, it promised an assemblage of parishioners to counter the increasingly Protestant hue of the white settlers, as well as an opportunity for members of the Oblate order to pursue their educational vocation. Accordingly, in 1896 the colony of St. Paul des Métis was established east of the Saddle Lake Indian Reserve, near the present site of St. Paul in east-central Alberta.[18] A board of management was formed, consisting of both Roman Catholic clergymen and federal politicians, and a priest was appointed as manager and representative of the board on the colony. Four townships were leased, plus two sections for the Oblate mission and school, at a nominal annual rent of one dollar. In addition, $2,000 was granted for the purchase of seed grain and implements. In the announcement of the project to the Metis, it was made clear that the land was completely under the direction of the Oblate missionaries and only destitute Metis need apply.

Thirty families moved onto the colony during its first year, and by the second year there were fifty families. The colonists were granted eighty-acre plots—title to which was retained by the Crown—but they were given no agricultural equipment or livestock. In spite of Father Lacombe's optimism, the colony was a dismal failure. It is perhaps an exaggeration to say that St. Paul des Métis was a "planned failure," but in retrospect one can see that it had little chance to succeed. Right from the beginning of the colony, the Oblates concentrated on their roles as administrators, teachers and religious leaders. They were neither predisposed nor competent to assist the Metis in establishing an agricultural community. Accordingly, they used the largest part of their limited financial resources to build a large boarding school (which later burnt, possibly the result of arson by some Metis children), church and presbytery. Moreover, it seems that the manager of the colony, Father Therien, was skeptical from the beginning about the prospects for "redeeming the half-breeds," and that he harboured the dream of creating a community of French Canadians at St. Paul. This is precisely what happened. In 1908 the board of management of the colony informed the government that it wished to terminate its leases. And in 1909, when the colony was terminated, some 250 French-Canadian claims on the former Metis lands were registered with suspicious haste.[19] Some Metis claims to the land were recognized, but within a few years most of the former Metis colonists had left the area.

While it is easy, and no doubt partly justified, to blame the clergy for the failure of St. Paul des Métis, the government cannot be absolved of its share of the guilt. The government either acted on the basis of expediency, employing half-hearted and cheap measures to deal with a profound problem, or it operated on the bizarre assumption that religious instruction was the principal means of transforming the "childlike" Metis into agriculturalists—or both. As we shall see, although the influence of the clergy diminished, the paternalistic attitudes of government officials and the white experts to whom they turned for advice remained intact during the hearings that led to the formation of the Metis settlements, and eventually in the legislation that governed the settlements.

During the two decades after the collapse of St. Paul des Métis no further schemes to better the lot of the Metis population were undertaken and, with the exception of a few who became successful farmers, their condition continued to deteriorate. The precarious situation of the worst-off Metis became desperate with the onset of the Great Depression which, in western Canada, was accompanied by an exceptionally severe drought. As many as half of Alberta's Metis were destitute and in dire need of government assistance. But the presence of a social need does not guarantee that it will be met. This was especially so in the Alberta of the 1920s and 1930s. Even before the advent of the Depression, the provincial and municipal governments, which bore major responsibility for the provision of relief, were having difficulty in meeting their responsibilities. As the Depression deepened, their finances were stretched to—and in some cases beyond—the breaking point. Moreover, Metis were not the only—nor in the eyes of the politicians the most important—people who were devastated by the Depression. It is worth considering, therefore, some of the reasons why the Metis eventually received the comparatively favourable treatment represented by the creation of the settlements.

The Metis Association of Alberta

Without doubt, a principal factor in the success of the Metis was the Metis Association of Alberta (MAA).[20] The MAA grew out of concerns expressed by a group of Metis squatters in a forest reserve at Fishing Lake, which is located in the extreme eastern area of central Alberta. Two factors concerned this group. First, in 1929 the forest reserve was to be opened to settlement, and the Metis were afraid that their lands would be lost. Second, control of natural resources in the prairie provinces was to be transferred from the federal to the provincial governments in 1930, and the group sought to have land reserved for its members before the transfer took place. Subsequent meetings in 1930 and 1931 drew larger attendance and wider representation, culminating in three major developments. First, councillors were elected from each Metis community in northern Alberta. Second, a petition containing over five hundred signatures asserting Metis demands for land, education, health care, and free hunting and fishing permits was presented to the provincial government. Third, in response to the Metis demands, the Department of Lands and Mines prepared a questionnaire to be circulated to as many Metis as possible by their elected councillors.

In December 1932, at a convention in St. Albert attended by delegates from all over the province, L'Association des Métis d'Alberta et des Territoires du Nord-Ouest was formally established. In a predominantly anglophone province, the organization soon assumed the name by which it is known to this day, the MAA. In the study of the evolution of organizations it is a common failing to devote excessive attention to leaders and to understate the importance of the rank and file. Nevertheless, the MAA was extremely well served by its earliest leaders. Three men played a prominent role: Joseph Dion (president), Malcolm Norris (first vice-president) and James Brady (secretary-treasurer).[21] They were exceptional not only in their individual talents and commitment but also in the remarkable complementarity of their abilities and dispositions. Dion, an enfranchised Indian and long-time teacher on the Kehewin Indian Reserve, was a devout Roman Catholic with ties to the clergy, and the most "respectable" of the three. This respectability was important since the leftist radicalism of Norris and Brady was distasteful to most Albertans. Norris's strength was his articulateness and exceptional skill as an orator in both Cree and English, while Brady was a consummate strategist and tactician. They regularly articulated and pressed on the provincial government the principal Metis demands: education for their children, medical care for their sick, free hunting and fishing permits for the pursuit of their livelihood and, above all, land. The vehement and persistent pressure exerted by the MAA was to bear fruit.

A second factor contributing to the success of the Metis was the support their cause received from certain Alberta politicians.[22] The involvement of white politicians began in earnest when the Liberal member of the Legislative Assembly (MLA) for St. Paul, Joseph Dechene, and his federal counterpart, Percy Davies, the Conservative member of Parliament (MP) for Athabasca, became involved in a game of one-upmanship in championing the Metis cause and courting the Metis vote. Dechene took the initiative, but Davies soon began to press Premier Brownlee, leader of the United Farmers of Alberta (UFA) government, for action on behalf of the Metis. Brownlee responded at first by insisting that responsibility for the Metis was at least partly federal and later by ignoring Davies's letters. Davies thereupon changed his tactics and induced D.M. Duggan, the Conservative house leader, to raise the issue in the Alberta legislature. Accusing the government of neglecting its responsibility for the health, education and general welfare of the Metis, Duggan moved a resolution in 1933 that a special committee of the legislature be appointed to inquire into "the whole half-breed situation," with consideration of "some plan of colonization of the half-breed population." Arguing that the complex problem of the Metis was already being examined by the government, Brownlee proposed an amendment to the resolution that was obviously a delaying tactic. This amendment would require the government only to continue its study "with a view to" presenting its recommendations at the next session of the legislature. To prevent this potentially embarrassing issue from being buried, Dechene proposed a subamendment which would require the government to present its recommendations within ten days of the beginning of the next session. The passage of this resolution, with Dechene's amendment intact, obliged the government to provide concrete proposals concerning the Metis.

The task of formulating proposals was turned over to the Department of Lands and Mines, of which R.G. Reid was the minister. The civil servants in that department pursued their investigation, consulted with the MAA, and tabulated the results of the questionnaire. Their finding was that the situation of the Metis was deplorable. The deputy minister mooted the possibility of establishing Metis reserves in areas of the province not sought by white settlers, but he maintained that the Department of Lands and Mines did not have the authority to examine the feasibility of this idea. Moreover, he pointed out that such a far-reaching decision would be a matter of policy, not of administration, and thus not the responsibility of civil servants. He recommended the appointment of a royal commission to investigate and make recommendations.

The cabinet, now led by R.G. Reid, accepted this advice. Before the royal commission was appointed, strenuous efforts were made to persuade the federal government to participate, and thereby accept some responsibility for remedying the plight of the Metis. However, the federal government insisted that the Metis were ordinary citizens who did not come under the Department of Indian Affairs, and that the responsibility of the Canadian government ended with the issuing of scrip.

While the pressure of the MAA and the jockeying of politicians for partisan advantage were the most powerful considerations, some additional factors contributed to the appointment of the royal commission, its recommendation that Metis "colonies" be established, and government's acceptance of this recommendation. First, the government was in financial difficulty. In the depths of the Depression, and in the face of the federal government's refusal to accept responsibility, any scheme that would involve large expenditures of money was distasteful. Setting aside land, especially in regions unsought by white settlers, was an attractive alternative. Second, there were precedents for using the allotment of land as a relief measure, such as St. Paul des Métis. But a more timely precedent was the cooperative project, begun in 1932, of the governments of Canada, Alberta and the city of Edmonton to resettle unemployed families with farming experience on land in northern Alberta.[23] Finally, by 1934 the UFA government was in serious trouble. Faced with an election in the next year, it was not blind to the threat of the Social Credit movement. In December 1934 an order in council was passed establishing a royal commission to inquire into "the problems of health, education and general welfare of the half-breed population of the Province."

The Ewing Commission

The royal commission consisted of three prominent Edmontonians. A.F. Ewing, the chairman, was a judge of the Supreme Court of Alberta and former Conservative MLA. E.A.Braithwaite was a doctor and provincial coroner who had played a prominent part in organizing the public health services in Alberta. J.M. Douglas, who had served as an MP and as alderman and mayor of Edmonton, was a stipendiary magistrate for the Northwest Territories. The findings and recommendations of the Ewing Commission, as it came to be called, were based on three sources of information and opinion: written testimony provided by government officials and the MAA; meetings held in a number of towns in central and northern Alberta and public hearings held in Edmonton. The most important of these was the public hearings held in Edmonton from February to May 1935.

A great deal has been made of the disagreements which surfaced during the Edmonton hearings.[24] Some of this disagreement centred on fundamental matters, and there were certainly conflicts between the commissioners and the MAA spokesmen, especially Malcolm Norris. The attitude of the commissioners toward the Metis spokesmen was condescending and often hostile. Moreover, comments about the Metis population by the commissioners and several witnesses were often paternalistic and racist, although it should be noted that the Metis leaders themselves were frequently paternalistic to some of their constituents.[25] However, it is a mistake to allow this discord to obscure the remarkable degree of consensus that underlay the hearings.

For one thing, it was generally acknowledged that a considerable segment of the Metis population was in dire straits: landless and poverty stricken, uneducated or undereducated, and disease ridden. As well, two distinctions among the Metis were generally accepted. The first of these was between Metis in the northern and those in the central parts of the province. The northern Metis were seen as capable of fending for themselves, pursuing a nomadic way of life and living off the land, while the Metis in central Alberta could not pursue the traditional ways because of the depletion of fish and game and the advance of white settlement. A second distinction was drawn within the Metis of central Alberta. Some members of this group, including the spokesmen for the MAA, had adapted to the advance of civilization and were able to cope in the dominant society and economy. The members of the other group were seen as childlike, undisciplined and improvident. It was also agreed that although the Metis had no legal right to special remedy, steps must be taken to better the condition of the destitute Metis and that it was the job of the government to do so. Finally, it was assumed throughout the hearings that the principal result of the commission would be the establishment of Metis settlements, although no mention was made of land settlements in the commission's terms of reference. The main goal sought by the Metis through the commission—endorsement of the establishment of a land base—was won without a fight.

This is not meant to suggest that the Ewing Commission hearings were congenial. In addition to their condescension the commissioners used a familiar political ploy for discrediting pressure group spokesmen—they expressed doubts about the extent of the Metis leaders' following. But friction was not just a matter of tone but also of substance. For instance, testimony presented by the MAA and corroborated by a High Prairie physician, claiming extraordinarily high rates of infant mortality, tuberculosis and venereal disease among the

Metis, was challenged by Dr. Harold Orr, director of the Social Hygiene Division of the Department of Health. Orr maintained that the incidence of tuberculosis and venereal disease amongst the Metis was only slightly higher than among the white population of the province. The reliability of Orr's testimony was challenged by the Metis spokesmen; he had once advised his minister against sending a doctor to Grouard because "the cost would be prohibitive unless the Venereal Disease Vote was very greatly increased."[26] Nevertheless, the commission's report suggests that it gave Orr's views some credence.

Education was another controversial area. The fact that 80 percent of the Metis population received no formal schooling was not in dispute. Disagreement arose, however, over how to remedy the situation and who should provide the remedy. Some of the Roman Catholic clergymen who testified at the hearings, as well as the commissioners themselves, believed that only the most rudimentary education was necessary or desirable for a people they saw as lacking either the inclination or the aptitude for other than the most elementary intellectual tasks. Bishop Guy of Grouard agreed with the Metis leaders that a substantial education was one of the principal needs of the Metis, and he proposed the establishment of land reserves which would house not only elementary schools but also residential schools for the children of parents who continued to be nomadic. But the question of who should provide the education was more controversial. The Roman Catholic clergymen argued vigorously for mission schools and although Joseph Dion, a devout Roman Catholic, might have accepted this, by the time of the Ewing Commission he appears to have been more a figurehead than a central decision-maker in the MAA; Malcolm Norris and James Brady were strongly anticlerical. Furthermore, the dismal failure of St. Paul des Metis, responsibility for which was widely attributed to the Roman Catholic Church, had not been forgotten.

Probably the most consequential disagreement that emerged during the Ewing Commission hearings had to do with the meaning of the term "Metis" or "half-breed." At the beginning of the Edmonton hearings, Ewing sought a working definition of the people under investigation. Malcolm Norris proposed that "if he has one drop of Indian blood in his veins and has not been assimilated into the social fabric of our civilization he is a Metis."[27] A few days later the following interchange took place:

> Ewing: Would you say the definition "anyone having Indian blood in their veins and living the normal life of a half-breed comes within the definition of "half-breed"?

Norris: Yes . . .

Ewing: You see, you must include "living the life of a half-breed" . . . there are a large number of men in Edmonton occupying responsible positions who are not intended to be included in this investigation.[28]

The clear implication of Ewing's words was that men "occupying responsible positions" were not "half-breeds," even if they could trace their ancestry to the Metis of the Red River, and even if they regarded themselves and were regarded by others as Metis. Ewing wished to confine to the destitute the category of persons eligible to reside on any land reserved for Metis; the destitute were those who lived a nomadic or seminomadic lifestyle and were mostly uneducated and in poor health. Accordingly, "half-breeds" were defined as people who failed to measure up to the standards of the dominant society. The principal political implication of this definition was that if "half-breeds" were childlike, they must be treated as children. Not surprisingly, the recommendations of the Ewing Commission and the subsequent legislation establishing the settlement associations were paternalistic, calling for government tutelage and supervision at almost every level.

Report of the Ewing Commission

The Ewing Commission submitted its report to the government on 15 February 1936. Only fifteen pages in length, it is in many respects a shoddy document. For example, the "long and interesting history [of the Metis] dating back almost to Confederation," including a discussion of the failure of scrip, was sketched in two pages. James Brady's estimate of the extent of communicable diseases was rejected without contrary evidence as "an overstatement," but his unverified estimate of the size of the Metis population ("about eleven thousand, of all ages") was reported without comment.[29] Although the commissioners visited a number of communities in north-central Alberta, they were only able to report that Metis living near white settlements "are *said to be* living in shacks on road allowances."[30] Concerning a disagreement over the nature and extent of education appropriate for Metis children, the report states that "no evidence was given on this point nor is the experience of the Commissioners sufficient to appraise the practical value of these arguments."[31] The commission apparently accepted the claim that in spite of the efforts of some denominational schools, 80 percent of Alberta Metis children received no schooling. This situation was attributed mainly to the nomadic disposition of the Metis people, and to the aversion of Metis children to endure ridicule and humiliation by the white children at public schools. In general, the report is replete with unsubstantiated assertions and speculative generalizations. No mention was made of the questionnaire prepared by the Department of Lands and Mines.

The Ewing Commission was assigned to inquire into "the health, education and general welfare of the half-breed population of the Province." In its report, it acknowledged that the Metis had serious health problems, which were attributed to several factors: the Metis generally lived far from doctors and nurses and lacked the money to visit them or pay for their services; the Metis were not visited by travelling doctors or nurses; unsanitary home conditions promoted the spread of various communicable diseases and sexual promiscuity propagated venereal disease; the Metis lacked proper food, and sometimes lacked food altogether. It was also acknowledged that the infant mortality rate was high among the Metis. Having acknowledged this, however, the report came to the following conclusion: "On the whole, the Commission is of the opinion that while the health situation is serious, it is not, except as to the particular diseases mentioned [presumably tuberculosis and venereal disease], more serious than among the white settlers."[32]

The commission observed the distinction, which had been emphasized by a number of witnesses at its Edmonton hearings, between residents of the north and central regions. While it acknowledged that the northerners lacked educational and health services, and that their shelter and clothing were inadequate, their ability to live off the land was emphasized. The real problem was seen to lie in the central region. In an uncharacteristically forthright statement, the commissioners allowed that "those half-breeds are said to be living in shacks on road allowances and eking out a miserable existence, shunned and suspected by the white population." The main problem in the central region was said to be the shortage of fish, game and fur-bearing animals.

How did the Metis arrive at their lamentable condition? At one point the commission report suggested a racist explanation, referring to "the admitted fact that the half-breed is *constitutionally* unable to compete with the white man in the race of modern life."[33] For the most part, however, the diagnosis centred on the Metis heritage. Their history as children of the fur trade was believed to have implanted in them a preference for the nomadic life, a propensity to live from day to day, and a distaste for a settled, agricultural existence. All of this made them easy targets for the land speculators who relieved them of their scrip, thereby depriving them of a haven when living off the land was no longer viable.

Having described and explained the condition of the Metis the report suggested measures to remedy the situation. Two constraints on any proposed remedies were stated early in the report. The first of these concerned the term "Metis." The commissioners stated that they were "not concerned with a technically correct definition."[34] They announced that:

> It is apparent to everyone that there are in this Province many persons of mixed blood (Indian and white) who have settled down as farmers, who are making a good living in that occupation and who do not need, nor do they desire, public assistance. The term as used in this report has no application to such men.[35]

A Metis was defined, for purposes of the report, as "a person of mixed blood, white and Indian, who lives the life of the ordinary Indian, and includes a non-treaty Indian."[36] In short, Metis who were successful by the standards of the dominant society did not qualify.

The second constraint concerned the basis of remedies proposed by the report. Early in the report the commissioners asserted that "the Government of this Province is now faced, not with a legal or contractual right, but with an actual condition of privation, penury, and suffering."[37] The commissioners insisted that assistance was not owed to the Metis as a matter of legal or even moral right. Government actions were to be based on "considerations of humanity and justice," not on aboriginal right.

In addition to these basic constraints, the commissioners formulated three guidelines for their recommendations. First, they rejected temporary relief measures based on considerations of individual need. They saw the problem as requiring "a comprehensive scheme which will go to its root and offer an ultimate solution." Second, they held that depressed economic conditions demanded that their recommendations should be inexpensive to implement: "All we can hope is to submit a relatively inexpensive scheme which would be capable of expansion in better times if time and experience show such expansion to be desirable."[38] Finally, the commission would not submit recommendations which would make the Metis, like Indians, wards of the government on the grounds that this would be too expensive and would impede initiative. It seems more likely that the commission wished to avoid any hint that special treatment for the Metis was a matter of right.

In order to grasp fully the import of the recommendations of the Ewing Commission, it is important to keep in mind not only the constraints and guidelines adopted by the commissioners but also their overall objective: "The logic of the situation would seem to be that he [the Metis] must either change his mode of life to conform with that of the white inhabitants or he must gradually disappear."[39] In concrete terms, the commissioners took this to mean that the Metis must become farmers and stock raisers or vanish. The alternatives were stark: either assimilate or disintegrate. It may be objected that segregation is an odd way to pursue an assimilationist policy, that the commissioners must have seen this, and that it is therefore a mistake to describe their goal as assimilationist. However, the commissioners had grounds for believing that segregation was a necessary step toward assimilation. In order to see this it is necessary only to recall three points in the commissioners' conception of the Metis. First, they saw the commitment of the Metis to their traditional ways, and their distaste for agriculture, as deep seated. Second, they saw the Metis as childlike and undisciplined, and therefore slow to learn new ways. Third, they saw the Metis as inevitable losers in competition with whites, and therefore proximity to white farmers would be discouraging and not conducive to assimilation. This outlook was stated quite clearly:

> A long process of education and training is necessary. A gradual initiation into the new life is the only possible way. It is during this long period of transition rendered necessary by the white man that he has a right to look to the white man and the white man's organized system of Government for help, for guidance, and for encouragement.[40]

The assimilationist objective was restated in the commissioners' preface to their recommendations. After expressing their opinion that "some form of farm colonies is the most effective, and, ultimately, the cheapest method of dealing with the problem," they stated: "We think... that over a long period of time the tendency will be to make the half-breed more and more dependent on farming and stock raising. This is the aim and purpose of the plan."[41]

The recommendations of the commission were straightforward. It was suggested that the plan be initiated by selecting two areas having the following characteristics:

> 1. The area should contain a very considerable amount of reasonably good agricultural land.

2. It should contain, or be adjacent to, a lake or lakes from which a supply of fish could be obtained.

3. It should have sufficient accessible timber suitable for the erection of log buildings.

4. If possible, the area should be capable of being enlarged if the scheme should require later expansion.

5. The area selected should be such as will be free from interference by white settlers.[42]

Since the principal objective of the plan was to convert the Metis to agriculture, each head of a family would be allotted a parcel of land, the size of which would be determined "by his capacity properly to use it."[43] Although title to the land would remain perpetually in the Crown, the allottee would be assured of continuous tenure for himself and his heirs, unless the land was forfeited by misconduct.[44] The government would supply a limited amount of farm machinery, to be used in common by the colonists under the supervision of an instructor, and the allottees would be taught farming, dairying and stock raising.[45]

It was suggested that a small hospital be built on each colony, which would periodically be visited by a doctor until a resident doctor became necessary.[46] Schools were also to be built, at which boys would be taught farming, girls sanitation, sewing and knitting, and all children reading, writing and elementary arithmetic.

Final control of the government of the colonies would rest with a government department.[47] Residency would be a privilege—no one would have the right to join a colony. Oddly, however, the commission proposed that any Metis who failed to join a colony "should have no claim for public assistance."[48] Day-to-day management of the colonies would be carried out by supervisors appointed by the government, in accordance with such regulations as the government found appropriate, and they would have the powers of police magistrates. Finally, provision would be made for councils elected by the members of the colonies, but such councils would have advisory powers only.

It would be unfair to characterize the Ewing Commission report as utterly inadequate. It did recognize the Metis as a unique group in Alberta society. It also proposed—within the limits of the commissioners' paternalistic and assimilationist assumptions—some humane steps for dealing with "the Metis problem." Above all, it recommended the first (and still the only) collective Metis land base in Canada. Nevertheless, the report was seriously defective in its inadequate compilation and analysis of factual evidence, and in its treatment of fundamental principles.

The basic problem lay in the fact that a fundamental ambiguity permeated the commission's treatment of the relationship between the Metis and the government. The core of the ambiguity had to do with the commission's recognition of the unique nature of the Metis. Throughout much of the report their uniqueness seemed to consist of their poverty, poor health and lack of education. Of course, the Metis were not unique in these respects. Many white settlers shared these debilities, and many persons of mixed Indian and white ancestry did not. If the Metis were in fact only victims of the Depression, they could have been dealt with by the same measures of relief granted to other citizens. That the commission did not recommend this was an implicit recognition that the Metis had something else in common—their propensity to pursue a common lifestyle. Only this common lifestyle could justify the recommendation that colonies be established exclusively for the Metis. The ambiguity here is that the Metis were characterized as *both* ordinary *and* special. Clearly the commissioners, while steadfastly opposed to granting the Metis special status like that of the Indians, were constrained to admit that the Metis were unique. This emerges most clearly in the recommendation that, while the Metis should not be compelled to join colonies, they would have no other claim to public assistance if they did not.

Another ambiguous point regarding the status of the Metis emerged in the report. Throughout the hearings of the commission, Ewing had suppressed any discussion of Metis history that might apportion blame for their plight to government policy. The Ewing Commission report itself stated that the plan recommended was a welfare scheme, which was not to be construed as satisfying the rights of the beneficiaries. However, near the end of the report a striking reversal takes place:

> The Commission is of opinion that as the Metis were the original inhabitants of these great unsettled areas and are dependent on wildlife and fish for their livelihood, they should be given the preference over non-residents in respect of fur, game and fish.[49]

In other words, the scheme proposed was a welfare measure but it also recognized the rights of the Metis as original inhabitants of the territory.

The significance of the ambiguity of the Ewing Commission report was not immediately apparent. However, its importance grew as the years passed, for it became increasingly clear that the strength of the

Metis claim to land and to self-government increased if it was based on right and not merely on government largesse.

Unlike its UFA predecessor, the new Social Credit government was under no pressure to respond to the concerns of the Metis. Accordingly, it took the government until November 1938 to respond to the recommendations of the Ewing Commission by passing the Metis Population Betterment Act.

The passivity of the Metis between the suppression of the North-West Rebellion and the onset of the Great Depression could well have been taken as confirmation of the view that the Metis could not withstand the pressures of white civilization. They were forced, it might have been thought, to become Indian or white. However, a remarkable resurgence occurred in which a formidable Metis organization was created almost overnight and a government forced once again to address the issue of land for the Metis. This phenomenon will be examined in subsequent chapters.

NOTES

1. The point is not to play on words. Sometimes the term "half-breed" is used to refer to "mixed-bloods" of British descent and "Metis" to refer to those of French descent. Riel himself occasionally used this distinction, although it is not obvious that he did so for reasons other than translation. In contrast, I used the terms "Metis" and "half-breed" interchangeably, so my point is that the conventional view is that the "mixed-blood" population was overwhelmingly French.
2. George F.G. Stanley, *The Birth of Western Canada: A History of the Riel Rebellions* (1936; reprint, Toronto: University of Toronto Press, 1961), viii.
3. See, for example, the essays in Jacqueline Peterson and Jennifer S.H. Brown, eds., *The New Peoples: Being and Becoming Metis in North America* (Winnipeg: The University of Manitoba Press, 1985).
4. My understanding of Metis history is particularly indebted to the following sources: Howard Adams, *Prison of Grass* (Toronto: New Press, 1975); Thomas Flanagan, *Riel and the Rebellion: 1885 Reconsidered* (Saskatoon: Western Producer Prairie Books, 1983); Marcel Giraud, *The Metis in the Canadian West*, 2 volumes (Edmonton: University of Alberta Press, 1986); Joseph K. Howard, *The Strange Empire of Louis Riel* (Toronto: Swan Publishing Company, 1952); W.L. Morton, *Manitoba, A History* (Toronto: University of Toronto Press, 1967); Donald Purich, *The Metis* (Toronto: James Lorimer & Company, 1988); Duke Redbird, *We Are Metis: A Metis View of the Development of a Native Canadian People* (Willowdale: Ontario Metis & Non Status Indian Association, 1980); D. Bruce Sealey and Antoine S. Lussier, *The Metis: Canada's Forgotten People* (Winnipeg: Pemmican Publications, 1975); and D.N. Sprague and R.P. Frye, *The Genealogy of the First Metis Nation* (Winnipeg: Pemmican Publications, 1983).
5. Jacqueline Peterson, "Many Roads to Red River," in Peterson and Brown, *The New Peoples*, 62.

6. Sealey and Lussier, *The Metis*, 29.
7. Ibid., chapter 11.
8. Trudy Nicks and Kenneth Morgan, "Grande Cache: The Historic Development of an Indigenous Alberta Metis Population," in Peterson and Brown, *The New Peoples*, 163-81.
9. Stanley, *The Birth of Western Canada*, 13.
10. See, for example, Irene M. Spry, "The Metis and the Mixed-Bloods of Rupert's Land Before 1870," in Peterson and Brown, *The New Peoples*, 95-118.
11. Redbird, *We Are Metis*, 5.
12. Little of what follows (the main exception is the discussion of the Ewing Commission report) is based on original research. Heavy reliance has been placed on the work of others, especially: the Metis Association of Alberta and Joe Sawchuk, Patricia Sawchuk and Theresa Ferguson, *Metis Land Rights in Alberta: A Political History* (Edmonton: Metis Association of Alberta, 1981); Murray Dobbin, *The One-and-a-Half Men* (Vancouver: New Star Books, 1981); Paul Driben, *We Are Metis: The Ethnography of a Halfbreed Community in Northern Alberta* (New York: AMS Press, 1985); and Judith Hill, "The Ewing Commission, 1935: A Case Study in Metis-Government Relations" (unpublished Honours essay, University of Alberta, 1977). The full extent of my indebtedness to these works is not completely acknowledged.
13. Driben, *We Are Metis: The Ethnography of a Halfbreed Community*, 31-33, 58.
14. The aptness of this comparison was suggested by Hill, "The Ewing Commission," 4-6.
15. Peter A. Cumming and Neil H. Mickenberg, eds., *Native Rights in Canada* (Toronto: Indian-Eskimo Association of Canada, 1972), 124-25.
16. A careful examination of scrip may be found in Metis Association of Alberta, *Metis Land Rights in Alberta*, chapters 4 and 5.
17. Cumming and Mickenberg, *Native Rights in Canada*, 7.
18. A thorough discussion of the rise and fall of St. Paul des Métis, on which this sketch is largely based, may be found in Metis Association of Alberta, *Metis Land Rights in Alberta*, chapter 5.
19. Ibid., 178.
20. On the early years of the MAA, see Dobbin, *The One-and-a-Half Men*, chapters 4 and 5; and Hill, "The Ewing Commission," chapter 1.
21. Dobbin, *The One-and-a-Half Men*, is a political biography of Brady and Norris, but it also casts a good deal of light on Dion and other Alberta Metis leaders. Hill, "The Ewing Commission," chapter 1, provides a brief but perceptive sketch of all three.
22. The role of the politicians is discussed in Hill, "The Ewing Commission," chapter 2.
23. Hill, "The Ewing Commission," 13.
24. All three of the works cited in note 12 are guilty on this score, in my judgment. I do not challenge the evidence they provide; indeed my own interpretation is based on that evidence.
25. This point is noted by Dobbin, *The One-and-a-Half Men*, 96 and 98-99.
26. Ibid., 101; Hill, "The Ewing Commission," 67.

27. Dobbin, *The One-and-a-half Men*, 95.
28. Ibid.
29. Report of the Ewing Commission, 5.
30. Ibid., 8 (emphasis added).
31. Ibid., 7.
32. Ibid., 5.
33. Ibid., 4 (emphasis added).
34. Ibid.
35. Ibid.
36. Ibid.
37. Ibid., 3.
38. Ibid., 9.
39. Ibid., 3-4.
40. Ibid., 4.
41. Ibid., 10.
42. Ibid., 11.
43. Ibid.
44. Ibid.
45. Ibid., 12-13.
46. Ibid., 14.
47. Ibid., 12.
48. Ibid., 12-13.
49. Ibid., 13.

2

Legal Status of the Alberta Metis Settlements

It would be impossible for any government to conduct all of its business strictly in accordance with the law. In the first place, the range of matters dealt with by governments is so extensive that a law which covered all of its activities would have to be impossibly detailed. Second, even when the law and supplementary regulations are comprehensive, unexpected contingencies arise which, in the name of common sense, expediency or justice, require that the letter of the law be stretched or even circumvented. Finally, every government organization has an informal code of conduct which supplements the "black letter law" under which it is supposed to operate. Among the most important of these unofficial rules are those which prescribe that various consultations take place before official action is taken. These extralegal norms of conduct are especially important in regard to the operation of the Alberta Metis settlements, for two interrelated reasons. First, the settlements have a peculiar relationship with the government of Alberta. Second, the legislation under which the settlement associations operate is seriously out of date. In fact, the act according to which the settlements are supposed to be governed, as well as the regulations made pursuant to that act, are currently under review.

The government of the Metis settlements is conducted under legislation known as the Metis Betterment Act as well as a considerable number of orders in council made pursuant to that act. Both the legislation and the regulations have changed over the years, and it is relevant to consider the more important of these changes. Two main criteria will be employed for determining whether or not a legislative change was important. First, did it engender serious controversy? Second, did it affect the movement of the settlements toward increased autonomy?

The Metis Betterment Act

The initial, brief act providing for the establishment and governance of the Metis settlements, the Metis Population Betterment Act, was promulgated on 22 November 1938. Since this was the first legislation governing the settlements, it is appropriate to summarize its main provisions.

The preamble to the act asserts that it is a response to the recommendations of the Ewing Commission and that "it is convenient and in the public interest that the ways and means of giving effect to such recommendations should be arrived at by means of conferences and negotiations between the Government of the Province and representatives of the Metis population of the Province."

The term "Metis" is defined in the act as a person of mixed white and Indian blood but excludes non-Status Indians as defined in the Indian Act. Administration of the act is assigned to the member of the executive council (cabinet minister) who is assigned that responsibility. The minister is authorized to cooperate with the board of any settlement association in formulating schemes for bettering the general welfare of the Metis, including the settlement of members of associations on lands set aside for that purpose by the province.

The lengthiest part of the act relates to the formation and government of associations of Metis to be settled on the land. First, it is specified that the minister responsible may promote the formation of one or more associations of Metis "who are unable to secure out of their own resources a reasonable standard of living." Second, it is required that the constitution and bylaws of such associations state the qualifications and conditions of membership, and that they make provision for the election, terms of office and procedures of a governing board of not more than five persons. Third, it is specified that the aims of such associations shall be to cooperate with the minister in formulating schemes for their betterment and for their settlement on lands set aside for that purpose by the province. Finally, it is provided that the constitution of any association is subject to the approval of the minister and may not be altered or amended without the minister's consent.

The act provides that any scheme formulated pursuant to it must be approved by the lieutenant governor in council (the cabinet). As well, the cabinet is empowered to set aside unoccupied provincial lands for Metis associations until such time as it is satisfied that "for any reason whatsoever the lands so set aside . . . are unsuitable or are not required for the settlement of any members of any such association." Finally, the act authorizes the cabinet to prohibit persons who are not members of a Metis association from hunting and trapping on land set aside for an association.

The first alteration of the act was the 1940 Act to Amend and Consolidate The Metis Population Betterment Act. In fact, however, the penultimate section of the 1940 act states that: "*The Metis Population Betterment Act*, being chapter 6 of the Statutes of Alberta, 1938 (Second Session), is hereby repealed." The most striking difference between the two acts is that the 1940 version is more than three times as long as that produced in 1938. It might appear that the difference between the two acts is not significant because most of the 1938 act is incorporated into the 1940 version, and because the later construction simply states some of the details of the government's already comprehensive authority over the settlements implicit in the earlier act. However, the 1940 act made some important changes, and the extensive additions it contained expressed an altered understanding of the relationship between the settlements and the government of Alberta.

This change in outlook is signalled by the omission in the 1940 act of the prefatory endorsement of "conferences and negotiations between the Government of the Province and representatives of the Metis population of the Province," and is embodied in the new sections of the act, almost all of which grant legal powers to the cabinet, to the minister with the approval of the cabinet, or to the minister alone. The sanctioned regulations are sweeping in scope. For example, one section of the act authorizes the minister, with the approval of the cabinet, to make regulations concerning such matters as "the buildings which may be erected upon any land allocated for occupation by a Settlement Association and to prohibit the erection of any buildings in contravention of any such regulations and to provide for the demolition or removal of any building erected in contravention of any such regulation." This section concludes by empowering the minister, with cabinet approval, "to make regulations as to any matter or thing not hereinbefore specifically mentioned which have for their purpose the advancement and betterment of any Settlement Association, or any of the members thereof, or the administration of the affairs of any Settlement Association, or of any land allocated to any Settlement Association." The minister is empowered to prescribe penalties for the breach of any regulation made under the act.

The Metis Betterment Act was consolidated in chapter 233 of the Revised Statutes of Alberta, 1970, with subsequent amendments. From the standpoint of government and politics, neither the 1970 consolidation nor subsequent amendments have altered the legal status of the settlements or their relationship to the provincial government. This means that the legislation governing the political life of the Metis settlements was largely in place by 1940, with no significant amendments since 1952.

Orders in Council

Numerous orders in council have been made pursuant to the Metis Population Betterment Act. The bulk of these deal with such matters as fishing, hunting, trapping, timber, the running at large of domestic animals, and the issuance of grazing leases. These regulations affect the daily lives of the residents of the settlements, but are only indirectly relevant to this study, which concentrates on government and politics. Their only obvious political relevance is that they reveal the extent to which the government of Alberta has seen fit to manage the settlements according to its own agenda. At this point, we consider only those orders in council which have either a direct bearing on the internal government of the settlements, or which have generated sustained controversy between the settlements and the provincial government. The pertinent regulations fall into three categories: those which deal with the formation and dissolution of settlement associations, and with the allocation of land within them; those which authorize and amend the constitutions of the settlement associations; and those which bear on the financial affairs of the settlements.

Settlement Land

Although the Ewing Commission had recommended that only two experimental colonies be initially established, a joint committee of Metis leaders and government officials identified twelve areas as available and suitable for Metis settlements. Subsequently, three of these were rejected: Pigeon Lake, on the grounds that the Metis had no interest in settling it; Marlboro, on the grounds that too many parcels of land in the area were reserved for other purposes; and Siebert Lake, on the grounds that it was encumbered by too many timber reservations. Seven others were established as Metis settlement association areas by various orders in council in 1938 and 1939. Subsequent orders in council added to and subtracted from the lands of the various settlements, and amalgamated and split some of them. There are currently eight settlements. Four are found in western Alberta, including Big Prairie, Gift Lake, East Prairie and Paddle Prairie. Four others are found in eastern Alberta, including Kikino, Elizabeth, Caslan (recently renamed Buffalo Lake) and Fishing Lake.

Two colonies, Wolf Lake and Cold Lake, were closed in 1960. Cold Lake was uninhabited, but Wolf Lake was shut down in spite of petitions by the residents. Its closure remains a bitter memory for many Metis, relating as it does to their principal political concern—the security of their land base. There appears to be ample statutory authority for the abolition or diminution of any settlement, since every version of the Metis Population Betterment Act has included a provision whereby the cabinet may "repossess" any settlement lands no longer deemed suitable or required for purposes of the act. On the other hand, however, Metis leaders point out that section 3 of the original act called on the minister responsible to "do such acts and things as he may consider proper for the purpose of co-operating with the Board of any association. . . ." Unilateral alteration of the boundaries of a settlement, they insist, is not cooperation.

Current regulations regarding allotment of land within a settlement are outlined in a 1960 order in council. The main provisions are:

>1. An applicant for a parcel of land on a Settlement must be a member of the Settlement Association in question.
>
>2. The application may be for an agricultural parcel of not less than twenty acres or for a village lot.
>
>3. The application must be approved by both the Board of the Settlement Association and the Minister responsible.
>
>4. The applicant must move onto the allotted land within thirty days of notification that the application has been approved.
>
>5. Within a year of approval of the application, the applicant must make certain specified improvements to the allocated land.
>
>6. Upon completion of the required improvements, the Settler is to be granted a Certificate of Occupancy, which constitutes title to the allotted land.
>
>7. Any member of a Settlement Association who resides for twelve consecutive months outside the colony, without the consent in writing of the Minister or his agent, forfeits membership in the Association and the right to land allotted to him.
>
>8. If the Board of a Settlement Association complains to the Minister that a Settler is interfering with the satisfactory working of the Association, the Minister may refer the complaint to the Attorney General for investigation. If the Attorney General finds the complaint to be well founded, the Minister may cancel the Certificate of Occupancy and may also cancel the Settler's membership in the Association.
>
>9. If the Minister finds that a Settler is not making proper use of a reasonable portion of the land allocated to him, the Minister may cancel the Settler's Certificate of Occupancy and issue another Certificate for a smaller parcel of land.
>
>10. No part of the land of a Metis Settlement is liable to seizure under legal process.

11. In the event of the death of a Settler, his land rights descend to his immediate family (widow and children).

12. Land may be allotted for a church, but no residence or school "of any nature whatsoever" may be built on land leased for church purposes.

13. Land allotted to settlers confers to them surface rights only.

Settlement Constitutions

Section 4 of the original Metis Population Betterment Act provided that the constitution of any settlement association "shall be subject to the approval of the Minister and when it is so approved, it shall be binding on all the members thereof," and that "the Board of any association may alter or amend its constitution only with the approval of the Minister, and any such alteration or amendment shall be of no force or effect until the same is approved by the Minister." The act states that a constitution must meet three requirements. First, it must specify the qualifications and conditions for membership in the settlement association. Second, it must vest control of the business and affairs of the association in a board consisting of not more than five persons and make provision for the election and terms of office of the members of this board. Third, it must specify "the manner in which the activities of the association shall be carried on." Pursuant to these statutory requirements, the various Metis settlement associations adopted identical constitutions at local meetings in 1939. In response to the requirement that qualifications for membership be specified, these constitutions stated that eligibility was confined to Metis of the full age of twenty-one years, who had resided in Alberta for a period of at least five years immediately prior to the date on which they made application for membership.

Several provisions were adopted to meet the requirement regarding the composition, manner of election, and terms of office of board members. Provision was made for either three- or five-person boards. In order to be eligible to serve on a board, a candidate had to be a Metis of the full age of twenty-one years, a member of the settlement association, and a resident of the settlement for at least one year prior to the election. Persons who had been convicted either of a crime punishable by imprisonment for two years or more, or of three minor offences punishable by imprisonment, were ineligible. Members of both three- and five-person boards were to be elected for three-year staggered terms. The presiding officer (and returning officer) for both nomination and election was to be an official designated by the Minister, who would cast the deciding ballot in case of a tie.

A number of provisions were adopted to satisfy the requirement that constitutions must prescribe the manner in which settlement business was to be conducted. A meeting of the board was to be held within three days of each annual election. At that meeting the board members were to elect one of their number as chairman for the succeeding year. A quorum of a board consisted of a majority of its entire membership. Boards could hold not less than four, nor more than twelve, ordinary meetings in each year. Ordinary meetings were to be held openly, with no member of the settlement association excluded except for improper conduct. Special meetings, however, could be held at any time, but all board members were to be present at such meetings. At every ordinary meeting, the date, time and place of the next meeting was to be set, and this information was to be communicated by the chairman, in writing, to any board member not present at the meeting. Each board could make rules and regulations for the calling of meetings, procedure within meetings, and other matters pertaining to the transaction of its business. The board could pass bylaws and regulations which became effective when approved by the minister. The initial constitution laid special duties and responsibilities on the chairman of each settlement association, who was designated "the chief executive officer of the Settlement Association."

In 1952, the Legislative Assembly amended part of the section of the Metis Betterment Act dealing with the constitutions of settlement associations. In the original act, it was prescribed that the constitution of a settlement association should provide for a board consisting of not more than five persons, and that it should make provision for election of the members of the board and their respective terms of office. The 1952 amendment drastically changed this provision. Thereafter, the chairman of the board was to be the local supervisor of the area appointed by the Metis Rehabilitation Branch of the Department of Public Welfare (that is, a civil servant ultimately answerable to the minister). The remaining four members of the now mandatory five-member board were to be members of the settlement association, but two of them were to be appointed by the minister, and only two elected by secret ballot. Two points may be made about this amendment. First, the new provision enhanced the ability of the provincial government to administer the settlements as it saw fit. Second, the amendment appeared to conflict with the spirit of the act's other provisions regarding settlement constitutions. These had indicated that the initiative for making and altering constitutions should come from the settlements, with the government either endorsing or rejecting such initiatives. Indeed, the subsection of the act which refers specifically to constitutional amendments states that "a board of a settlement association may alter or amend the constitution of the settlement association only with the *approval* of the Minister, and such alteration or amendment has no force or effect until it is *approved* by the Minister" (emphasis added). Settlement leaders have maintained that the boards propose amendments, whereas the minister merely gives or withholds consent, while the government can appeal to the provision of the act granting the minister the broad authority "to make regulations as to any matter or thing not hereinbefore specifically mentioned which have for their purpose the advancement and betterment of any Settlement Association, or any of the members thereof, or the administration of the affairs of any Settlement Association, or of any land allocated to any Settlement Association."

It would appear that we are confronted here with an unresolved legal dispute. The settlements maintain that the act states clearly that constitutional amendment may be accomplished through a proposal by a settlement board and approval by the minister. The government claims that this customary manner of making amendments can be overridden by the act's assignment to the minister of overruling responsibility for the betterment of the settlements.

This disagreement was intensified by the appearance in 1966 of another order in council relating to settlement constitutions. Many of the provisions of this regulation simply reaffirm the *status quo ante*, and most of the changes are regarded by residents of the settlements as innocuous or desirable. For example, the regulation reduces to eighteen from twenty-one the age at which settlers may vote for, and serve on, settlement boards; provides for by-elections to fill vacancies on boards; requires that regular meetings of boards be held monthly; and provides for remuneration of the members and secretaries of boards. However, it contains one very contentious provision, providing that the board of a settlement association "shall consist of three members, all of whom shall be elected by the members of the Colony." This provision is problematical in two ways. First, it conflicts with the current provision of the Metis Betterment Act, described above, according to which a board must consist of five persons, of whom three are to be appointed. This contradiction between the prevailing law and the prevailing regulation controlling the constitution of boards raises questions about the validity of the acts of any board, however it is constituted. Second, and of greater practical political importance, the regulation, like the statutory amendment with which it conflicts, was imposed on the settlements without consultation or consent. To settlement political leaders, this means that the only legally valid constitutional provisions relating to the settlements are the original ones, which were adopted by the colonies in 1939 and approved by orders in council in 1940 and 1941. They regard subsequent amendments not only as evidence of bad faith on the part of government, but as illegal. This does not contribute to the spirit of trust and cooperation between Metis leaders and governmental officials which would facilitate Metis betterment.

One final point needs to be made about the constitutions of the Metis settlements. The settlement associations, unlike municipalities, are not corporations: they do not have the rights, powers and privileges of legal persons. This is a serious disability which emerges most dramatically in the ongoing litigation between the settlements and the provincial government over the ownership of subsurface resources in the settlement areas. There are important day-to-day consequences as well. Lacking the standing to sue or be sued, settlement boards have had to resort to very imperfect devices in their dealings both with governments and with private enterprises.

Finances

Residents of Metis settlements, their liability to taxation and their right to have public funds expended on their behalf, are in many respects identical to their neighbours outside the settlement areas. In some respects, however, the fiscal position within the settlement differs from that on the outside. There are two important provisions concerning finances in the Metis Betterment Act itself. Subsections 5-8 of section 9 exempt members of settlement associations from all acts which provide for the assessment and taxation of land, but they permit the provincial cabinet to establish a tax in lieu of other land taxes and empower the minister to enforce the collection of this tax. Section 18 protects the real and personal property of settlers—except for goods sold under a valid conditional sale agreement—from seizure under legal action. In other words, the only legal remedy available to the creditors of defaulting Metis settlers is to repossess goods sold on a "rental purchase" basis. It is easy to see that this is a mixed blessing: the advantage of the protection it affords is countered by the disadvantage that lenders are understandably reluctant to enter into agreements with Metis settlers.

The provision for taxation in lieu of the standard taxes was implemented in 1960 by Order in Council 466:

> Every member of a Settlement Association who has, for the time being, the exclusive right of occupation of any allotment in any Metis Colony, shall pay to the Minister each and every year by way of tax, an amount equivalent to 25 mills on an assessed value of Four Hundred Dollars ($400.00) for each allotment held by said member. Every member to be given the privilege of working out this tax on any community project authorized by the Supervisor of Metis Rehabilitation, at the current wages being paid for such work, or by the delivery to the Local Supervisor of the Colony, the equivalent value of sawlogs, pulpwood, or firewood.

The option of a nonmonetary payment, known as the "annual levy," was important in earlier days but is no longer exercised. The regulation's lack of clarity is one of the reasons why the current act and the regulations pertaining to it are under review. Two problems with the regulation suffice for purposes of illustration. First, does the regulation say that the assessed value of each allotment is to be $400, so that the annual levy remains $10 per year in perpetuity, or does it allow for periodic reassessment? If the latter is the correct interpretation, who is to perform the assessment, according to what criteria, and with what avenue(s) of appeal for those assessed? Second, what constitutes an allotment for purposes of the regulation? Initial allocations of land ordinarily consist of one quarter section or one lot in a hamlet. But active farmers and ranchers often receive several additional allotments. It was recommended by the Ewing Commission, and it is the policy of the settlement councils (as the boards referred to in the act are called) that settlers should be allotted as much land as they can use productively. Thus the following question arises: does an allotment consist of the totality of the land a settler has been allocated, or does each quarter section constitute a separate allotment? According to one interpretation, a settler allotted a parcel in a hamlet and two sections of land could be required to pay an annual levy of only $10, but another interpretation woul have him pay a levy well in excess of $300.

Turning now from provisions concerned primarily with taxation to those concerned primarily with revenue, we find only one legal obligation in the Metis Betterment Act itself, and it is implied rather than stated. The first substantive provision of the act states that the minister "may do such acts and things as he considers proper for the purpose of co-operating with the board of a settlement association . . . to formulate one or more schemes . . . to better the general welfare of the Metis population of the province." Although the provision says "may" rather than "shall," the fact that the point of the act was to promote the betterment of the Metis through the formation of colonies, and the advancement of self-sufficiency by means of cooperative schemes on the colonies, strongly suggests that the act enunciates a legal obligation, and not a mere permission, for the provincial government to contribute financially to the betterment of the settlements; the provincial government has in practice contributed hundreds of thousands of dollars out of general revenue to the settlements over the years.

The financial provision which has caused the most heated controversy between the settlements and the provincial government, and which constitutes perhaps the most serious impediment to a more constructive and cooperative relationship between the two, involves a 1960 order in council. This regulation established the Metis Population Trust Account, to be held by the provincial treasurer, from which the minister may authorize expenditures for the betterment of settlement associations. The bulk of the revenue of the trust account is to be acquired from timber dues, grazing leases and hay permits, surface rights compensation from oil companies, "*and all moneys received from the sale or lease of any other of the natural resources of the [settlement] areas*" (emphasis added). In some respects, the trust account has been quite beneficial to the settlements. Revenue, especially from surface rights compensation, has been considerable, and although the minister must authorize expenditures from the fund, it provides a source of revenue that cannot be regarded as government largesse.

Nevertheless, the regulation soured relations between the settlements and the provincial government. The italicized phrase quoted above states that one source of revenue accruing to the trust account is all moneys derived from the sale or lease of any of the natural resources of the settlement areas, other than those specifically mentioned in the regulation. Thus the settlements maintain that the trust account should receive the revenues derived from the sale or lease of subsurface, as well as surface, natural resources. The provincial government, however, maintains that subsurface rights on Crown land remain the property of the Crown. Both sides are intransigent and the settlements are currently suing the province of Alberta for the rights to mines and minerals on the settlements. The financial stakes in this litigation are high, for the Settlements could gain $100 million from oil and gas sales. Protracted examinations for discovery are now under way, and there is little prospect that the case will be decided in the near future. The political circumstances surrounding the initiation of this suit, and the political consequences of pursuing it, will be examined in subsequent chapters.

3

Government and Politics of the Metis Settlements: An Overview

This chapter will examine the Alberta Metis settlements, paying closer attention to political realities than to formal legal requirements. The actors having a more or less significant effect on the government and politics of the settlements will be identified and described. The purpose here is to provide an overview of the organizations and officials which influence the pattern of politics in the settlements. Genuine analysis of the government and politics of the settlements does not begin until the following chapter, in which we begin to examine more closely the interrelationships among the three organizations which have the greatest political impact in the settlements: the settlement councils, the FMSA and the MDB. For the time being, we sketch the structure, authority and activities of these organizations only in broad strokes, along with other, less influential organizations. The present chapter therefore has a second limitation in addition to its primarily descriptive rather than analytical character, in that it is concerned almost exclusively with what political scientists and sociologists call organized political elites. That is, it concentrates on groups and agencies that specialize in political and/or administrative activities, neglecting individuals and groups whose political activity is more sporadic and less intense. This means, in particular, that we largely ignore, for the time being, the political behaviour of the ordinary residents of the settlements.

For purposes of orderly exposition, the following discussion will treat the settlement councils as the main focus of attention. Priority will be given to providing a more politically realistic description of the structure and functions of the councils; other groups and agencies are discussed in the context of their relationship to the councils.

Although consistently referred to in legislation and orders in council as "boards," the governing bodies of the Alberta Metis settlement associations are now invariably called settlement councils. Each of the eight councils consists of five members, one of whom is chairman. Council members are elected for three-year staggered terms, with two elected in one year, two the next, and one in the third. If a council member leaves office before the next annual election, a by-election is held. Elections are conducted by secret ballot, and all residents who are members of the settlement association, and who are eighteen years of age and over, are entitled to vote.

The powers and responsibilities of the settlement councils can be distinguished usefully into three types: general, specific, and informal. The general powers and responsibilities of a settlement council stem from two sources. First, each version of the Metis Population Betterment Act has specified that a central purpose of the settlement associations is to cooperate with the responsible minister in devising plans and projects for the betterment of the settlements; the settlement council is to be the main representative of the settlement associations in these activities. Second, by virtue of being the duly elected government of a settlement association, the council is responsible for doing whatever is necessary, proper and possible to increase the well-being of those it governs.

The general powers and responsibilities of a settlement council involve it in both internal and external spheres of activity. Internal activities are those in which it engages as the government of a community. Given a certain level of resources, the council takes steps to enhance the facilities, services and opportunities available to members of the settlement association. In an attempt to ensure that continuous attention is given to matters of concern to the residents, councils in recent years have allocated "portfolios" (such as housing, agriculture, recreation, and economic development) among their members. Even areas of council activity which might seem uncontroversial can be quite contentious and time-consuming. Consider, for example, the area of recreation. The decision whether to improve the community hall for dances and bingo games, buy new uniforms for the hockey teams, develop a picnic ground, upgrade the baseball diamond, improve the beach, hire a recreation director or adopt some combination of these alternatives can arouse heated debate. Such debates are exacerbated by the fact that the Metis settlements suffer from appallingly high levels of unemployment. Thus projects that promise even temporary jobs for some of the settlers, such as improving the baseball field, have priority over those that do not, such as buying team uniforms, regardless of strictly recreational considerations. Moreover, even a choice among job-creating recreational projects invites controversy. The decision to appoint a recreation director gives one person a relatively remunerative and long-lasting source of income; the decision to develop a picnic site gives many people temporary and low-paid employment; and the decision to improve the community hall provides temporary, relatively well-paid work to a few skilled and semiskilled adults.

In recent years money has been made available to the settlement councils to hire staff, to the extent that they may now be said to have small corps of civil servants of their own. Each has a settlement manager, who is supposed to exercise broad supervisory authority, keep abreast of the availability of government programs, and perform specific tasks assigned by council. Each has at least one secretary-receptionist and one full- or part-time bookkeeper. Some of the settlements have made major purchases of heavy equipment and hired a person to manage it. Some have full-time recreation directors. One has developed a game-ranching operation which employs a manager and other workers. All employ foremen for their house-building and repair programs, and caretakers for their community buildings. In addition, supervisors and foremen are employed from time to time on a temporary basis to oversee various projects. The upshot of this is that now one of the general governmental functions of the settlement councils is that of exercising general direction over a small civil service.

The external general activities of a settlement council are those which involve it in relationships with organizations and individuals outside the settlement. Councils interact with both government and nongovernment agencies. The most important of the government organizations for the settlement councils has been the MDB of the Department of Municipal Affairs. It consisted of a director, two managers and seven staff members in its central office in Edmonton, a manager and small staff in its western district office in High Prairie and its eastern district office in St. Paul, and a small regional office to serve the Paddle Prairie settlement in the far north. Although the MDB gradually lost the high degree of authority over the settlements which it once possessed, it continued to surpass any other government agency in its impact on the settlements. In part, the centrality of the MDB derived from law. By order in council under the Metis Population Betterment Act, bylaws and regulations passed by a settlement council become effective only "when approved by the Minister [of Municipal Affairs]." Unless a bylaw involves the expenditure of a considerable amount of money, in which case higher-ranking officials in the Department of Municipal Affairs or even the minister could become involved, the authority to approve or disapprove rested with the MDB. Furthermore, as the only bureaucratic agency which specialized in, and which was expected to be familiar with the settlements, the MDB served as a clearing house for relationships between the settlements and the various provincial government agencies with which they dealt. For example, requests by settlements for services from other government departments were regularly referred to the branch for assessment. However, the MDB lost its position as the settlements' sole route of access to the provincial government. Settlement councils frequently appeal directly to an assistant deputy minister (ADM) of Municipal Affairs. The councils also have regular dealings with a number of government departments, especially Agriculture, Education, Advanced Education, Housing, Manpower, Attorney General, Recreation and Parks (particularly its Fish and Wildlife Division), and Transportation.

Settlement councils interact with a number of nongovernmental agencies and individuals, the most important of which is the Alberta FMSA. Composed of one representative from each of the settlement councils and a four-person executive elected at large, the federation performs several services on behalf of the councils. The person who carries the main responsibility for providing these services is the president of the FMSA, who is a full-time paid officer, assisted by a small clerical, administrative and research staff. The most important functions performed by the FMSA are those associated with its role as the main pressure group for the settlements. Under the general direction of the FMSA's board the president, sometimes in association with one or more board members, presses various agencies of the provincial government to provide facilities and services deemed beneficial to the settlements. The FMSA lobbies extensively on subjects ranging from the revision of the Metis Population Betterment Act to securing specialized training programs for settlers. The FMSA also serves as an important forum for the exchange of information and ideas. The president of the FMSA and his staff provide the settlement councils with advice and information, while meetings allow councillors from the various settlements to share ideas and information. This sharing of ideas and information is also facilitated by occasional "all council meetings," composed of all the council members from all the settlements as well as the executive members of the FMSA. Finally, in addition to its structured, "rational" efforts to set worthwhile and practical goals and to devise efficient and effective means to attain them, the FMSA is an important instrument for morale; its meetings remind council members that they are not alone in facing formidable difficulties.

Although the president of the FMSA exercises some discretion over how he performs his job, he cannot refuse to follow the board's directives, nor can he take bold initiatives without the board's authorization. The same is true of an institution known as Settlement Sooniyaw (*sooniyaw* is the Cree word for money). Settlement Sooniyaw is a corporation wholly owned by the settlements and designed to promote their economic development. Like the FMSA, the board of directors of Settlement Sooniyaw is composed of representatives of the settlements, but board members need not be members of the settlement councils. Although it is not yet a body of central political importance for the settlement councils, Settlement Sooniyaw will likely assume a position of major importance in the future, particularly if the litigation over subsurface mineral rights is resolved in favour of the settlements, or if an out-of-court settlement is reached, resulting in a considerable cash flow to Settlement Sooniyaw.

As has been mentioned, the Alberta Metis settlements constitute the only collective Metis land base in Canada. The MAA aspires to represent all Metis in the province, but especially those who are not members of settlement associations. Accordingly, the organization of the MAA is quite different from that of either the settlement councils or the FMSA. The basic unit of the MAA is the Metis "local," of which there are dozens in both urban and rural areas of the province. Locals are registered as societies under the Alberta Societies Act and must consist of at least ten members. The province is divided into six zones, and the governing body of the MAA is its board of directors, which consists of two directors elected by each zone, plus a president who is elected provincially. Matters of provincial concern, such as most research, lobbying at the higher levels of the provincial government, and participation in and liaison with other Native organizations, are carried on at the central office in Edmonton by the president and his staff.

In the past, the relationship between the Metis settlements and the MAA was constant and intimate. The leaders of the MAA played an indispensable role in the formation and the early administration of the settlements. In turn, the settlements were the principal evidence of the MAA's success. In recent years, however, the relationship between the settlement councils and the FMSA on the one hand, and the MAA on the other, have not been continuously harmonious. For its part, the MAA claims that while there are approximately fifty thousand Metis in the province, many of them in dire straits, the settlement councils and the FMSA have been content to protect their own privileged positions with little regard for their less fortunate cousins. The settlement councils and the FMSA counter this charge on three grounds. First, they maintain that the lot of the settlements is hardly enviable and that maintaining, let alone enhancing, the well-being of the settlers is extremely time-consuming. Second, they hold that the MAA has undertaken the responsibility of furthering the interests of off-settlement Metis and that entry into this sphere by the settlement councils and the FMSA would be an unwarranted intrusion. Third, they maintain that they do exhibit an appropriate concern for other Metis by offering available land on the settlements to qualified Metis and by demonstrating what can be done by Metis with a collective land base. Participation in the MAA by members of settlement associations has declined in recent years. In the summer of 1984, interviews were conducted with thirty-three of forty members of the settlement councils. Twenty-eight (85 percent) had once been members of the MAA, but at the time of the interview only thirteen (39 percent) were still members. During the same period residents of two settlements, one eastern and one western, were interviewed. In the eastern settlement, 68 percent of the voting-age respondents had been members of the MAA but only 44 percent remained members. In the western settlement, the corresponding figures were 77 percent and 50 percent. The typical response of those who had allowed their membership in the MAA to lapse was not an expression of hostility but a view that the MAA had little relevance to the settlements. However, many respondents felt that the settlement councils should cooperate with the MAA, and a vocal minority favoured increased efforts to bring about a more cooperative relationship.

The relationship between the settlement councils, the FMSA and the MAA, on the other hand, is not fundamentally antagonistic. Perhaps the best evidence of harmony and the potential for more cooperation in the future lies in the FMSA's relationship with the Metis National Council (MNC). The MNC is an alliance of the Metis associations in the three prairie provinces. In 1983, at the height of the deliberations about the application to Native peoples of the recently patriated constitution, the FMSA was granted a place on the constitution committee of the MNC, with authority to speak on matters relating to the existing Metis collective land base. Given the formal structure and the power relationships within the MNC, the FMSA could not have acquired a place on the constitutional committee without some good will between it and the MAA.

The specific powers and responsibilities of settlement councils mentioned earlier are those stated in the Metis Betterment Act, and the regulations made pursuant to that act. In keeping with the purpose of this chapter to move towards a more politically realistic sketch of the position of the councils, we will look now at some important ways in which the councils have in practice amplified, and in some cases modified, the rules and regulations under which they are legally supposed to operate.

The councils are empowered to pass regulations and bylaws for the settlements, subject to approval by the minister, but there is no legislation governing the procedure to be followed in adopting bylaws. The procedure actually employed is a somewhat democratized adaptation of the system characteristic of legislative bodies in the English-speaking liberal democracies. A proposed bylaw is brought before the council for first reading on a motion moved by one councillor and seconded by another. The discussion of the proposal at first reading is confined to its general merits; its details are not considered. If a proposal is supported by a majority of the council members it moves to second reading. At second reading, the details of the proposal are examined and amendments may be adopted. If one or more details in a proposed bylaw are found especially problematical, they may be referred to a committee for further study. If a proposal passes second reading, it is referred to a general meeting of the settlement association. If a proposal is supported by a general meeting (by a three-quarters majority), it proceeds to third reading. After this, the proposed bylaw is forwarded for ministerial approval, and when this approval is given the proposal becomes an official bylaw of the association.

General meetings, which all voting-age members of a settlement association are entitled to attend, are not provided for in the Metis Betterment Act or the regulations pursuant to it, but all the settlements have incorporated endorsement by a general meeting as part of the procedure for enacting bylaws, so that there is a *de facto* requirement that at least one general meeting be held each year. The agendas of general meetings are not confined to the consideration of proposed bylaws. Participants are free to ask council members questions about, and to criticize, the council's activities. Such questioning and criticism is not confined to matters of broad policy. The council members themselves may take the opportunity afforded by general meetings to assess the views of the settlers either on matters of long-range policy or on specific, immediate issues. Except when very controversial matters are to be discussed, attendance tends to be quite low, but general meetings nevertheless enhance the democratic character of the politics of the settlement associations.

The Metis Betterment Act states that the constitutions and bylaws of a Metis settlement association shall prescribe the qualifications for acquiring and maintaining membership in an association. The constitution states these qualifications:

> Those eligible to become members of a Settlement Association and to vote in the election of the board of such Settlement Association shall be confined to Metis of the full age of 18 years who have resided in Alberta for a period of at least 5 years.

Although this provision leaves the councils a good deal of discretion concerning admittance to membership, most of the criteria employed in granting or denying membership do not engender controversy. For example, there is a general consensus that settlers' adult children, born and raised on the settlement, should be given preference over outsiders. Also, it is generally agreed that new applicants should not be accepted unless there is land available for them which is accessible by road. Following this rule, some of the settlements have placed temporary freezes on membership. There is also general support for the policy of rejecting applicants who apparently intend to use the settlement only as a temporary residence to lower their cost of living, rather than a permanent residence. However, one of the criteria used by some settlements for rejecting applicants for membership is very controversial. In the eastern settlements the major source of livelihood for some of the settlers is the raising of livestock. For this purpose, extensive grazing leases have been granted on land that could be used to house settlers. There is a dispute between those who believe that the grazing areas should be reduced in size, thereby opening more land for habitation, and those who believe retention of the large leases is indispensable to the vital purpose of maintaining a viable agricultural sector. So far, the settlement councils have supported the latter view, but the controversy continues.

The settlement councils exercise a wide range of specific powers in addition to those described above. Here, however, there is a close correspondence between the councils' legal authority and their actual practice. Accordingly, we may turn to the final category of powers and responsibilities of the settlement councils, which have been labelled "informal." Informal powers are a residual category in that they derive neither from a government's general status as the government of a particular community nor from specific legal requirements and permissions. These informal powers and responsibilities owe their existence on the settlements mainly to the facts that the communities are small in population, geographically isolated and culturally distinct. As a result, members of settlement councils are called upon to perform both advisory and police functions.

Council members are regularly asked by their constituents for information, advice and assistance which, in larger and less isolated communities, would ordinarily be sought from civil servants or voluntary agencies. They are expected by their constituents to be both well informed and judicious in their assessment of the programs, services and opportunities provided by the provincial and federal governments and the private sector, as well as those for which they are specifically responsible.

Council members also perform informal police functions. The nature and burden of this task should not be exaggerated. Council members do not attempt, nor are they expected, to act as a general surrogate for the Royal Canadian Mounted Police (RCMP). However, council members are frequently called upon to intervene in minor incidents or threats of unlawful conduct, such as teenage vandalism and disturbances of the peace. Moreover, some council members become at least peripherally involved in police work because some RCMP detachments refuse to dispatch constables to a settlement unless requested to do so by a council member.

Since the purpose of this chapter is to shift attention from formal legal requirements to political realities, it is appropriate to conclude with a brief discussion of the pivotal role of the chairmen of the settlement councils. As was noted in Chapter 2, the original constitutions of the settlement associations explicitly recognize that the council chairman has powers and responsibilities over and above those involved in being one of the five members of the governing body of the settlement:

> *Duties of the Chairman of the Board*—He shall be the chief executive officer of the Settlement Association and shall
>
> (a) cause the laws, rules and regulations governing the Settlement Association to be duly executed;
>
> (b) cause correct records to be kept of all proceedings at all meetings of the Settlement Association and of the Board;
>
> (c) control and regulate all matters of procedure and form and adjourn the meeting to a time named;
>
> (d) so far as may be within this power, cause all negligence, carelessness and violation of duty to be duly prosecuted and punished;
>
> (e) report and certify all by-laws and other acts and proceedings of the Board to the Minister;

(f) to communicate from time to time to the Board all such information and recommendation [sic] such measures as may tend to better the welfare of the Settlement Association;

(g) to keep a correct list of all who are members of the Settlement Association.

Since the settlements now have some civil servants of their own the council chairman need no longer perform strictly clerical duties. However, the presence of these civil servants adds a new burden of supervision and personnel administration. Moreover, the list of duties stated in the original constitution does not include the off-settlement responsibilities—especially meetings with government officials in Edmonton and participation in the affairs of the FMSA—which occupy an increasing portion of an effective chairman's time. But the central role of the chairman derives from the fact that he is looked to for leadership by members of the settlement association, by fellow members of council, and by outside agencies. He is expected to have a comprehensive understanding of the current situation and future prospects of the settlement, and ideas on how its well-being can be enhanced. He is expected to be the principal spokesman of the council, both within the settlement and in its dealings with outside agencies, and he is expected to take primary responsibility for directing the settlement's staff. The importance of the council chairman is clear when he presides over a weak council. When, for whatever reasons, a council is weak, its effectiveness may depend almost entirely on the ability and enthusiasm of the chairman.

4

Councillors of the Metis Settlements

In Chapter 3 we moved beyond formal, legal description towards a more realistic examination of the government and politics of the Metis settlements. However, only a broad overview of the nature and functioning of the settlement councils, and the governmental and nongovernmental actors that influence them, was presented there. Here, and in the next two chapters, we will examine in some detail the three agencies which exceed all others in their impact on the government and politics of the settlements: the settlement councils, the FMSA and the MDB. Although these chapters are more realistic than the preceding one, they continue to ignore a crucial component of a fully realistic account—the ordinary residents of the settlements. We continue in these chapters to concentrate on political elites, the highly visible participants in the political process for whom politics and administration are central preoccupations. The serious limitation involved in confining attention to elites will be remedied in Chapters 7 and 8, where the political attitudes and activities of the "rank-and-file" residents of the settlements will be examined.

There are two main respects in which this chapter brings greater breadth and depth to the study of which it is a part. First, it reveals something of the social characteristics and political attitudes and opinions of the councillors of the Metis settlements. Second, it begins to discuss some of the main issues that absorb the attention of the councillors, as well as FMSA politicians and provincial government officials. We begin in this chapter with the settlement councils; Chapter 5 will examine the FMSA and the MDB will be considered in Chapter 6.

Basis of the Discussion

The following discussion of some of the characteristics and views of the members of the settlement councils is based on interviews conducted by the author in the summer of 1984. All interviews were conducted at the respondents' home settlements and respondents were guaranteed anonymity. All names used in this study, either of persons or of places, are pseudonyms. Thirty-three of forty councillors were interviewed. Two of the six councillors who were not interviewed were members of the northernmost settlement, which the author was only able to visit once. No more than one councillor was missed at any other settlement, and there were no striking differences (age, sex, or expressed or implied unwillingness to be interviewed) between the councillors who were interviewed and those who were not. The interviews, with two exceptions, were lengthy and frank; the shorter interviews were with respondents who had been recently elected to council with no previous experience. An interview form was used, and all the questions on it were asked initially as phrased. However, questions were subsequently rephrased and respondents were encouraged to pursue lines of thought suggested to them by the questions. The result was that almost all questions were answered.

Social Composition of the Settlement Councils

Twenty-eight of the councillors interviewed were male and five were female (85 percent versus 15 percent). Of the councillors not interviewed, five were male and two were female; thus, total numbers of thirty-three male councillors and seven female (82 percent versus 18 percent). This proportion of female elected officials is comparatively high for Canadian governments.

Table 1
Age of Metis Settlement Councillors, 1984

Age	Number	Percentage	Cumulative Percentage
Under 25	0	0.0	0.0
25-29	3	9.1	9.1
30-34	10	30.3	39.4
35-39	3	9.1	48.5
40-44	7	21.2	69.7
45-49	3	9.1	78.8
50-54	4	12.1	90.0
55-59	1	3.0	93.9
60-64	1	3.0	96.9
Over 64	1	3.0	99.9
Total	33	99.9	99.9

Note: In this table and others percentages may not add up to 100 due to rounding.

Ten of the councillors interviewed (30 percent) were born in the settlements they represented, and another seventeen (52 percent) had lived in their settlements for more than twenty years. Of the remaining six councillors, three (9 percent) had lived on their settlements for more than ten years, and the other three for more than five years.

There is considerably more variation in the ages of the councillors than in their duration of residence, as Table 1 indicates. Two features of this age profile should be noted, since they will be discussed later. First, the largest single group of councillors consists of people who are in their early thirties. Second, there are hardly any councillors who are elderly or in their late middle age.

There was also a considerable diversity as to the amount of formal education received by the councillors, as indicated in Table 2. The largest category, "some secondary," ranges from completion of grade 8 to near-completion of grade 12. There is a tendency for younger councillors to have more schooling than older ones. It is likely that this tendency will not only continue but intensify, since many settlers believe that to negotiate effectively with government officials and promote economic development, more formal education is now required than was formerly the case.

Table 2
Formal Education of Metis Settlement Councillors, 1984

Amount of Schooling	Number	Percentage
Some elementary	6	18.2
Completed elementary	2	6.1
Some secondary	21	63.6
Completed secondary	2	6.1
Some postsecondary	2	6.1
Postsecondary degree	0	0.0
Total	33	100.1

Twenty-nine of the thirty-three councillors (88 percent) were receiving income from employment other than their work as councillors, a very large proportion in areas suffering from extraordinarily high levels of unemployment. Their occupations were too diverse to be presented usefully in tabular form, but four generalizations can be made. First, the most common occupations were connected with farming and ranching. Second, most of the jobs held by those not involved in farming and ranching would be categorized as semiskilled. Third, a majority of the councillors, especially in the western settlements, did not have full-time, year-round jobs. In some cases this was due to the unavailability of such work, but more commonly, especially in the west, it was an expression of the continuing vitality of a way of life in which hunting, fishing and gathering remain culturally and economically significant. Finally, no councillors, even the most successful farmers and ranchers and the few who commuted to larger centres of population, were financially wealthy. A handful of settlers lived in a fashion comparable to the urban middle class, but the councillors (with one exception) were not among them.

Almost all of the councillors interviewed (twenty-eight of thirty-three) spoke fluent Cree, and only three confessed to having no competence at all in the language. There was no connection between facility in Cree and age: all but one of the councillors under the age of 35 was a fluent speaker. Native language retention (or its acquisition by young people who spoke no Cree) was a matter of importance for a few councillors, although none ranked it as a high priority. No connection was found between facility in Cree and political attitudes and opinions, including attitudes about the design of school curricula.

All but two of the thirty-three respondents described themselves as affiliated to a church or other religious community. The question was phrased in such a way as to encourage practitioners of traditional Indian religion to count themselves as having a religious affiliation; one respondent fell into this category. Of the two exceptions, one described himself as a nondenominational Christian who attends various churches irregularly, and the other had no religious beliefs or affiliations. The others were all Christians and predominantly Roman Catholic (twenty-seven of thirty). The Christian councillors were about evenly divided among those who described themselves as strongly religious, somewhat religious, and not very religious. No relationship was found between either the nature of respondents' religious affiliations or the strength of their religious convictions, and their political attitudes and opinions.

Twenty-two (66 percent) of the councillors interviewed had served on the council previously, many of them for several terms, although not always consecutively. Moreover, fifteen (46 percent) had served at least one term as council chairman. Thus, the typical council includes members who have had a good deal of experience. On the other hand, one-third of the council members had been elected for the first time only shortly before interviews began. Two brief comments about the new councillors are appropriate here, as they suggest something about the attitudes and opinions of the councillors and those they represent. First, almost all of the new councillors were relatively younger people added to relatively older councils or relatively older people added to relatively younger councils. There is a widely shared view on the settlements that this sort of "balance" is a highly desirable feature of a council. Second, four of the eleven new councillors were women, and there is a view on some settlements that it would be desirable if a higher proportion of the councillors were female.

Political Attitudes and Opinions of Settlement Councillors

The remainder of this chapter is concerned with the political attitudes and opinions of the council members, as well as some of the main political issues that absorb their attention. As we commonly speak, the terms "attitudes" and "opinions" are regarded as *private* possessions of those who hold them, whereas "issues" are regarded as *public* business, typically involving matters of controversy. This difference suggests that attitudes and opinions should be treated separately from issues. However, further reflection reveals that a sharp distinction is quite misleading. On the one hand, there is no such thing as an issue that is not *seen* as an issue: issues arise when and only when people differ in their attitudes and opinions. On the other hand, attitudes and opinions are activated, and sometimes changed, by the evolution of issues. Accordingly, our discussion of the opinions and attitudes of the councillors of the Metis settlements is at the same time a discussion of the issues that absorb the councillors—as well as the FMSA, the MDB, and many residents of the settlements.

Orientations to the Federal Government

In response to the question, "Do you usually vote in federal elections?," twenty-six of the thirty-three councillors interviewed (79 percent) answered in the affirmative. Twenty-three (70 percent) said that they had voted in the most recent federal election (1980); the voter turnout for the whole of Alberta was 61 percent. Table 3 shows the voting by party of these councillors. The pattern of voting differs somewhat from that of Alberta as a whole and from that of the areas of Alberta in which the settlements are located. The percentages of Conservative and New Democratic Party (NDP) voters are noticeably, but not strikingly, below average. Definitely striking, however, is the number of respondents who did not disclose their votes. Based on the behaviour of these respondents when asked about their federal votes (hesitancy, references to poor memory), combined with their openness about their provincial voting, it would appear that in fact they had not voted. The overwhelming majority of respondents claimed to be consistent supporters of the party they had voted for in 1980.

A number of unsolicited comments indicated that the general attitude of the councillors towards federal government politicians and civil servants is favourable. Several councillors indicated that their MPs kept up their constituency work and noted, with a combination of surprise and appreciation, that the MPs were more visible between elections than during campaigns. A number of councillors also commended federal civil servants for helpfulness, promptness and courtesy.

Table 3
Party Voting of Councillors, 1980 Federal Election

Political Party	Number	Percentage
Progressive Conservative	13	57.0
Liberal	6	26.0
NDP	1	4.0
No Answer	3	13.0
Total	23	100.0

The RCMP, about whom the councillors were questioned at some length, received mixed but generally favourable reviews. None of the councillors complained of harassment, seeing their settlements, if anything, as underpoliced. Moreover, only one complained of police racism, and in that case the problem was not seen as one of overt discriminatory mistreatment but of undue suspicion concerning the comings and goings of Native people, especially in the nearby towns. The most favourable opinions of the police were offered by the councillors of a settlement close to a town with an RCMP detachment, joined to that town by a paved provincial road, and with a cadre of Metis special constables training to become regular members of the RCMP. In addition to strongly favourable assessments of the performance of their standard duties—regular patrolling, prompt and courteous response to calls, and so on—the police of this detachment were commended for conducting well-conceived workshops for the youth of the settlement, and for keeping the council well informed about police activities.

At the other extreme, the councillors of a settlement distant from an RCMP detachment, and linked only by a very rough gravel road, were most unhappy about the quality of policing they received. These councillors saw their settlement, and the nearby Indian reserve, as dangerously underpoliced. They said that these communities were almost never patrolled on weekends, and that weekend calls for assistance were rarely answered before Monday. All of these councillors expressed the belief that the police were afraid to intervene in the often violent weekend conflicts within and between the Metis and Indian communities. They refused to blame individual police officers for their reluctance to enter these frays, but were incensed at policy makers who refused to locate an RCMP officer on the settlement, despite council's offer to build a good, well-furnished house, surrounded by a compound, for the use of such an officer. Their esteem for RCMP decision makers was not enhanced when a small detachment was subsequently located in another (predominantly non-Native and comparatively peaceful) isolated community.

The two situations described above are both atypical extremes, but they suggest the actual pattern of settlement councillors' attitudes towards the RCMP. Individual officers are generally held in high regard and are seen as trying to do a good job—or at least the best job possible under difficult circumstances. But complaints about police *effectiveness* increase directly with isolation from the nearest detachment. Although we have only one instance as a basis for forming a judgement, the Metis special constable program has been greeted with such enthusiasm that it surely merits extension. Metis councillors do not hate the police: they would prefer to see more of them than less.

Orientations to the Provincial Government

In response to the question, "Do you usually vote in provincial elections?," twenty-seven of the thirty-three councillors interviewed (82 percent) answered in the affirmative. Twenty-six (79 percent) said that they had voted in the most recent provincial election (1982); the provincial rate of turnout was 66 percent. Table 4 discloses the voting by party of the councillors who voted in the 1982 Alberta provincial election. Their pattern of voting differs significantly from the provincial average in only two respects. First, their preference for the NDP was significantly higher than the provincial norm (27 percent versus 19 percent), but closer to the norm for the northern part of the province, where the NDP runs much more strongly than south of Edmonton. Second, the Western Canada Concept (WCC) received around 12 percent of the provincial vote and assorted other right-wing movements around 4 percent, but there was only one professed WCC voter among the councillors (the WCC did quite well electorally in parts of the province where some of the settlements are located). The councillors were also asked if they generally supported the party for which they voted in the 1982 election. There were two noteworthy results. First, some of the older councillors, most of whom voted Conservative in 1982, recalled that they were once steadfast Liberals. Second, a number of councillors who said that they voted NDP indicated that they had previously supported other parties, most commonly the Progressive Conservatives.

Comments about local MLAs and provincial civil servants were generally favourable. Remarks about the MLAs, which were unsolicited but numerous, indicated that they were very attentive and helpful to their Metis settlement constituents, regardless of the proximity of elections; nineteen (58 percent) of the councillors described their MLAs as "especially helpful." Interestingly, the two warmest endorsements of the MLAs (all of whom are Progressive Conservatives) were given by an elderly councillor who was a long-time member of the Liberal party, and a young, ideologically committed member of the NDP.

Table 4
Party Voting of Councillors, 1982 Provincial Election

Political Party	Number	Percentage
Progressive Conservative	17	65.0
NDP	7	27.0
Liberal	1	4.0
Western Canada Concept	1	4.0
Total	26	100.0

The agencies of the provincial government were generally commended. Nineteen (58 percent) of the respondents said that all of them were very helpful, twelve (36 percent) that some were helpful and some not, while only one said none were helpful; one recently elected councillor with no previous experience expressed no opinion. The Department of Transportation, which is responsible for road-building and maintenance, received both the highest praise and the strongest condemnation. The praise was not localized, but the blame was confined to two settlements, one of which complained of a shortage of roads and the other of poor quality roads. The roads in both settlements are sources of friction between the councillors, their constituents and the provincial government. The Fish and Wildlife Division of the Department of Forestry is held in low regard by some councillors, especially in one of the western settlements in which a number of settlers rely heavily on fishing for their livelihood. Their view is that some of the officers of this division are less sensitive to the needs of the settlers than to the preferences of recreational anglers. Finally, some of the more experienced councillors see the Department of the Attorney General as creating needless obstructions to cooperation between the settlements and the provincial government, under the guise of not jeopardizing the government's position in its litigation with the settlements.

Orientations Towards the Metis Association of Alberta

The leaders of the Metis settlements have had an ambivalent relationship with the leaders of the MAA for several years. In this respect, it is interesting to note the pattern of MAA membership by councillors of the settlements, now and in the past. At the time of writing, only thirteen (39 percent) of the councillors interviewed were members of the MAA. Another fifteen (45 percent) were not currently members but had been in the past. Only five (15 percent) had never been members. The proportion of councillors who were members of the MAA had dropped substantially, but there is no obvious pattern (age, sex, political experience, geographical location) of membership or non-membership in the MAA. In particular, there is no significant relationship between age and MAA membership. In fact, the largest number of current members of the MAA is in the 30-34 age group, and the largest number of former members who have allowed their affiliation to lapse are over fifty years old. There is no case to be made, on the basis of the data presented here, that support for the MAA is based on old loyalties or nostalgia, and that its salience for settlement councillors will disappear as younger councillors supplant older ones. In fact, the matter of support for the MAA is a potentially serious issue for the individual settlements, and perhaps more particularly for the FMSA. There is a faction that sees the MAA as, at best, irrelevant to the concerns of the settlements and, at worst, as a meddlesome interloper into affairs that the settlements and the federation can handle quite satisfactorily without assistance. There is also a faction that largely accepts the unflattering assessment by MAA activists of the parochialism of many settlement leaders. Although strong words have been expressed by members of both factions, in personal interviews and in more public settings, neither faction has coalesced into anything resembling a caucus. It remains to be seen if the issue will disappear.

Councillors' Views on Their Roles as Settlement Politicians

This section will examine the councillors' views of their roles as political leaders in their own settlements. The discussion is divided into two parts. First, the councillors' feelings about their political positions and activities, concentrating on the rewards and burdens of office as they see them, will be considered. Second, their views concerning the issues they see as most important to the well-being of their settlements will be examined.

Each councillor interviewed was asked the following question: "Do you enjoy serving on council, on the whole?" Not surprisingly, in view of the fact that they sought election, thirty-one of thirty-three (94 percent) answered in the affirmative. They were then asked why they enjoyed their jobs, and what they found to be the most satisfying part of the job. The answers to these questions were so varied that any attempt to quantify them would be misleading, especially since the respondents were encouraged to give more than one answer if they wished. At the one extreme, some responses were very personal, in the sense that they said as much or more about the personality characteristics of the respondents than about the realm of government and politics (for example, "The job is challenging, and I can't resist a challenge"). At the other extreme, most responses were comparatively impersonal, in the sense that they referred primarily to the well-being of the settlement as a whole (for example, "To make the settlement a better place to live"). Between these extremes, and offered mainly though not exclusively by the more experienced councillors, were responses that related fairly specific personal qualities to matters of community concern. For example, some councillors spoke of their ability in, and the gratification they received from, negotiating with politicians and civil servants for particular benefits for their own settlement or all the settlements. Some found their main rewards in effectively handling their particular portfolios (education, recreation, housing). And a few saw themselves as outspoken advocates for particular groups within their settlements, such as the elderly, women and youth.

The respondents were next asked what they saw as the most difficult part of the job. Although a majority of councillors gave no answer to this question, either because they were too new to the position to identify any task as particularly trying or because they were simply unable to rank their duties in order of difficulty, the more experienced councillors had definite ideas about the relative difficulty of their various responsibilities. Leading the way by a large margin were duties connected with the allocation of scarce and highly valued resources among the residents. A difficult task for any politician, for many Native leaders it is extremely so, due to the profound importance of family and kinship ties in their culture. This point was stated poignantly by a council chairman: "By far the toughest part of my job is having to say 'No' to in-laws." Five councillors (15 percent) stated that unwarranted criticism by settlers, almost invariably related to ignorance of policies concerning the allocation of scarce goods, was the most difficult thing they had to deal with. Four others (12 percent) said that the most difficult part of of the job was explaining to settlers that, for reasons beyond the control of council, there was not and never would be an unlimited supply of houses, wells, jobs, and other scarce goods. When asked if there were any parts of the job they did not like, only nine councillors (12 percent) responded in the affirmative. The objects of their distaste were, again, quite varied, with some respondents saying that there was more than one aspect of the job they disliked. However, most of the respondents disliked dealing with the provincial government in general and the MDB in particular.

Two more findings concerning the councillors' feelings about their jobs are worth reporting. First, the councillors were asked if they thought that their colleagues on council took their jobs seriously enough. Sixteen (49 percent) responded in the affirmative, fourteen (42 percent) in the negative, two (6 percent) felt they had too little experience on council to answer the question, and one (3 percent) refused to answer. Those who found fault with their colleagues did so for two main reasons. Ten of the fourteen councillors who found shortcomings in some of their colleagues believed the latter violated proper standards of impartiality by favouring, or attempting to favour, friends and relatives. The other, less frequent, reason for condemnation involved what may be called parochialism. Some councillors believed that certain of their colleagues cheated their constituents by their unwillingness to leave the settlement in order to confront provincial government officials or to involve themselves in the activities of the FMSA.

Second, in an attempt to elicit a kind of summary expression of the councillors' commitment to their political vocation, each was asked: "Do you think you'll run for council again?" Eighteen (55 percent) responded in the affirmative, twelve (36 percent) were undecided, and three (9 percent) responded in the negative. All affirmative respondents were forceful and unequivocal, expressing a delight in politics both as a form of self-expression and as a worthwhile means of public service. Two of the negative respondents planned to retire at the next election for reasons of ill health; the other, who had served on council and numerous other community organizations for many years, felt it was time for younger people to take up the burden. Of the twelve undecided respondents, five had been elected to council for the first time only recently and felt it was too early to tell if they could perform well enough to seek reelection. Another four, all middle-aged, said that they would run again if they thought they were needed on council to provide experience and continuity. Of the remaining three, one said that he would run again if it appeared that the people wished him to do so; a second (the council chairman noted earlier as saying that he did not enjoy serving on council) said that he would not run if a capable settlement administrator were hired, but otherwise would run in order to contribute his experience in dealing with government officials to the council; the third, who was the youngest councillor interviewed, was deeply torn between inclination and duty, feeling that council responsibilities infringed upon the more carefree life he had been accustomed to living.

Councillors' Views on Local Issues

The focus of attention will now shift from the general political attitudes and opinions of the councillors to their positions on issues. First to be considered are "substantive" issues, which bear directly on the well-being of the settlers. Second, "organizational" issues, which have to do with the structure of settlement government, will be examined.

Table 5
Greatest Perceived Problem of Settlement, 1984

Greatest Problem	Number	Percentage
Unemployment	8	24.2
Housing	5	15.2
Lack of funding for economic development	3	9.1
Education	3	9.1
Metis Development Branch	2	6.1
Litigation	2	6.1
Lack of collateral	2	6.1
Insecurity of land	2	6.1
Other	6	18.0
Total	33	100.0

Each of the councillors interviewed was asked the following question: "What is the biggest problem facing your settlement nowadays?" Their responses were even more diverse than they appear in Table 5, since the categories in that table are quite compressed. In particular, "education" refers to one or more of poor quality of teaching, excessive drop-out rate, distance to school and shortage of adult education services; "housing" refers either to a shortage of accommodation, poor quality of existing housing stock, or both. Three terms in the table require brief explanation. "Litigation" refers to the suit brought against the government of Alberta by the settlements regarding the ownership of subsurface resources. "Lack of collateral" refers to the fact that both the settlement councils (not being legal corporations) and the residents of the settlements (not being freehold owners of their plots of land or houses) have great difficulty in putting up collateral for loans. "Insecurity of land" refers to the fact that the legal title of the settlements to their land is tenuous. Several years ago the Wolf Lake settlement was unilaterally terminated by the provincial government, and there is some fear that the same fate could befall any or all of the remaining settlements.

Concern with the problems of unemployment and housing is striking. However, the most surprising feature of the table is the size of the "Other" category. Where possible, all responses were fitted into a category containing more than one respondent, and still almost one in five of the councillors had a unique view of the biggest problem facing his or her settlement.

The councillors were then asked what was the second-greatest problem facing their settlement. Their responses are presented in Table 6. When these responses are combined with those presented in Table 5, it can be seen how seriously the councillors view the problem of unemployment; 45 percent saw unemployment as either the greatest or the second-greatest problem facing their communities. Two of every three councillors saw either unemployment or housing as the greatest or second-greatest problem.

Table 6
Second-Greatest Perceived Problem of Settlement, 1984

Second-Greatest Problem	Number	Percentage
Unemployment	7	21.2
Roads	3	9.1
Alcohol and drug abuse	3	9.1
Metis Development Branch	3	9.1
Housing	2	6.1
Lack of funding for economic development	2	6.1
Education	2	6.1
Litigation	2	6.1
Other	7	21.2
Total	33	100.0

Finally, each councillor was asked if there was any other major problem facing his or her settlement. This question elicited only two noteworthy responses. First, thirteen (39 percent) of the respondents identified no additional important problem. Second, the question added six councillors to the number of those who saw housing as an important problem, and two to those who saw unemployment as a major concern. In Chapter 8 we will see whether or not the councillors' assessments of major problems facing the settlements coincide with those of their constituents.

Two organizational issues relating to the government and politics of the settlements will now be considered. First, the councillors' views on the role of elders in the political life of the settlements will be examined. Second, their views on the proper extent of political independence of the settlements will be addressed.

Elders are held in almost as high esteem by the Metis as by their Indian cousins, the main difference being that the Metis, overwhelmingly Christian, do not assign to their elders so prominent a spiritual role. The proper political role of elders is an issue both in the settlements and in the FMSA. As a result of discussions in a number of forums, it was proposed that each settlement should establish a senate of elders to advise the council, especially regarding admission of new members to the settlement association and allocation of housing. At the time the interviews were conducted, two settlements had already established informal senates of elders.

Before raising the specific issue of the proposed senates, an attempt was made to obtain a general idea of the councillors' views concerning the appropriate political role of elders by posing the following question: "What do you think of the amount of attention given to the advice of elders in running the settlement; is it too much, too little, or about right?" Four of the councillors (12 percent) said that the elders had too much influence; nineteen (58 percent) said they had too little; nine (27 percent) said that they had an appropriate amount of influence; and one felt unable to answer the question. This array of opinions does not suggest that the political role of elders is a major concern for councillors. With 58 percent favouring an enhanced political role for the elders and only 12 percent favouring a diminution, the matter would seem to be closed. This impression is confirmed by the councillors' replies to the specific question: "Would you like to see a senate of elders established to advise the council?" Twenty-seven (82 percent) responded in the affirmative, while only six (18 percent) responded in the negative. However, these figures do not reveal the intensity of the opinions on the two sides of the question, and particularly on the "negative" side. All the opponents of an increased political role for the elders vehemently expressed the idea as stated by one councillor: "We have old people but no elders." Taking the accepted position that "eldership" is a matter of wisdom and not merely of age, the opponents maintained that, with few exceptions, the settlement elders were merely traditionalists, obsessed with "the good old days" and lacking the insight and foresight to bring traditional ideas to bear on new problems and opportunities.

The intensity of feeling expressed by the opponents of an increased political role for the elders suggests that the issue may be more serious than numbers indicate. Nevertheless, it is likely that the majority will prevail and that it will do so without creating deep animosities, since none of the opponents of placing greater political authority in the hands of elders was hostile to what may be called "the institution of eldership."

None rejected the idea that *real* elders should have a powerful political presence, and none showed any sympathy for the contemporary Euro-Canadian view that most people's capacities diminish rapidly after late middle age. Thus, their opposition was not to an increase in the political influence of elders as such, but to an increase in the political authority of "bogus" elders. They will likely be swayed by the argument that, in the nature of things, "genuine" elders, whose counsel will be eminently worth heeding, will emerge sooner rather than later.

Table 7
Councillors' Positions on Greater Political Independence for Settlements, 1984

Settlements better off if more independent	Number	Percentage
Yes	16	48.5
Qualified yes	9	27.3
Qualified no	3	9.1
No	5	15.2
Totals	33	100.1

At the time when councillors were being interviewed, self-government had already emerged as a central, if not *the* central, issue for Indian and Inuit politicians. Metis leaders, especially in the settlements, were more preoccupied with issues concerning land, and tended to avoid the term "self-government" as suggesting sovereignty or sovereignty-association, which played no part in their plans or aspirations. However, they were not indifferent to questions about the degree of independence from the provincial government that would be appropriate for the settlements. Accordingly, each councillor was asked the following question: "Would your settlement be better off if it were freer to make its own decisions without government interference?" The question was intentionally phrased in these broad terms, avoiding explicit use of the provocative term "self-government." Respondents were left as free as possible to interpret the question as they saw fit, and those who chose to understand it as referring to "self-government" were not discouraged from doing so. The responses to this question are presented in Table 7. It would have been misleading to categorize the responses as simply "yes" or "no," since a number of respondents were careful to qualify their answers, attaching conditions to their support for, or opposition to, greater political self-determination for the settlements. All of the respondents who gave qualified answers did so on pragmatic grounds. Without exception, those who answered with a qualified "yes" maintained that there should be a gradual movement towards greater autonomy, concomitant with an improvement in the quality of settlement councillors and administrators, with no definite degree of independence established as an objective to be achieved. In very similar fashion, those who answered with a qualified "no" held out the possibility that the settlements might soon develop the political and administrative capacities to take some short steps towards greater independence. Those who opposed greater political independence for the settlements maintained that it would open the floodgates to favouritism in general and nepotism in particular. Those who favoured greater independence maintained that the settlement councils, in consultation with their electorates, are better able than officials of the MDB to identify the needs and aspirations of the settlements, and to devise effective means to satisfy them.

5

The Alberta Federation of Metis Settlement Associations

The principal focus of this chapter is on the Alberta FMSA, which is involved in certain basic and far-reaching issues concerning the Metis settlements. Some issues regarding the status of settlement lands and the nature and scope of the governmental jurisdiction of the settlements have entangled the FMSA in major agreements and disagreements, negotiations and even litigation, which have involved the participation of senior civil servants, cabinet ministers and premiers. Accordingly, before examining the structure and operation of the FMSA, a brief outline of the major background issues will be provided.

Major Background Issues

As with leaders of the other groups designated as aboriginal peoples in the Constitution Act, 1982, the central concerns of the Metis politicians are land and enhanced political self-determination. Moreover, like the other groups, the Metis moved from seeing security of land tenure as the most important concern to seeing it as related to a greater scope of self-government. As far as the Alberta Metis settlements are concerned, neither the issue of land nor the issue of self-government could be addressed alone by such a small agency as the MDB. Furthermore, in view of the opposition of both the Lougheed and the Getty governments to constitutional entrenchment of "undefined and unspecified aboriginal rights," such matters would have to be handled delicately, at the highest levels, as issues of fundamental government policy.

The security of land tenure has always been a concern of the settlements, particularly since the closure of the Wolf Lake and Cold Lake settlements in 1960. However, the emergence of land and self-government as issues central to the relationship between the settlements (with the FMSA as their representative) and the provincial government can be dated to the initiation of the lawsuit by the settlements against the province in 1977 (see Chapter 2).[1] This litigation engendered an ugly incident in 1979 between the settlements and the provincial government. Early one morning, representatives of the MDB appeared simultaneously at all eight settlement offices, seized documents deemed relevant to the litigation, and took the files to Edmonton. Although the Metis (as well as many others) were outraged by this high-handed action, the seizure of the documents had one positive consequence. Discussions between the FMSA and the government led to an investigation by the Alberta ombudsman, who recommended that a committee be established to review and recommend changes to the Metis Population Betterment Act and the regulations made pursuant to it.

The government passed an order in council in 1982 establishing the Joint Metis-Government Committee, which was charged with reviewing the Metis Betterment Act and reporting to the minister of Municipal Affairs. The committee was chaired by a former lieutenant governor of Alberta, Dr. Grant MacEwan, and included the president and another member of the board of directors of the FMSA, a government backbencher, and a representative designated by the minister of Municipal Affairs (the ADM to whom the MDB reports). The committee's terms of reference were quite broad, extending beyond a review of the Metis Betterment Act to include "a review of the current political, health, educational, cultural and economic situation on the Metis Settlements . . . the development of models in terms of local government, land holding, social organization and economic opportunity on Metis Settlements . . . [and] the establishment of guiding principles for the drafting of legislation which would allow for political, cultural, social and economic development on Metis Settlements."[2] The main thrust of the committee's report, which was delivered in the summer of 1984, is captured in a short passage in MacEwan's letter of transmittal:

> I would like you to know that one of the main concerns of our Committee has been the largely paternal nature of the 1938 Act. We have done our best to ensure that any proposals for a new Act would place the major responsibility for the political, social, economic and cultural development of the Settlements firmly on the shoulders of the Settlements themselves.

The committee recommended that fee simple title to the surface of the land of each settlement (without prejudice to the litigation regarding subsurface rights) should be vested in the settlement. Finally, although a number of the committee's other recommendations simply removed legislative contradictions and brought the law into conformity with well-established practice, certain recommendations significantly altered the structure and expanded the powers of the settlement councils.

In April 1985, at the third of the first ministers' conferences on constitutional matters affecting aboriginal peoples, agreement was reached between representatives of the FMSA and the Alberta government on a "made in Alberta" approach to constitutional entrenchment of settlement land and political rights. Under this approach, the rights in question would be entrenched by way of an amendment to the Alberta Act, which is part of the Constitution of Canada, after certain prerequisites agreed upon by the two sides were satisfied. The first stage in this process was completed on 3 June 1985, when Premier Peter Lougheed introduced a "Resolution Concerning an Amendment to the Alberta Act" to the Alberta Legislative Assembly. The resolution, which passed unanimously, requires the completion of two major tasks before a constitutional amendment is sought. First, the Metis are called upon to define and propose "fair and democratic criteria for membership in settlement associations and for settlement lands allocation to individual members of settlement associations" and "the composition of democratic governing bodies for the management and governance of Metis Settlements." Second, the government is called upon to propose to the legislature a revised Metis Betterment Act, incorporating appropriate standards for membership, land allocation and democratic government in the settlements. A constitutional amendment would be proposed only after the government and the settlements agreed on a revised Metis Betterment Act.

Board of Directors of the FMSA

The FMSA was incorporated as a nonprofit society under the Alberta Societies Act in 1975.[3] According to the FMSA's bylaws, its membership consists of all the settlement councils which choose to participate in its meetings. In fact, however, most of the FMSA's work is done by its board of directors, which consists of twelve people: one director representing each settlement, and a four-member executive council consisting of a president, vice-president, secretary, and treasurer. Ordinarily, the director representing a settlement council is its chairman, but another member of the settlement council may be designated to assume the position, either temporarily or for as long as the council wishes.

The members of the executive council are elected at an annual meeting by the settlement councillors. Voting is by secret ballot, with each settlement having one vote. Election requires an absolute majority of all the votes cast. The president and the secretary are elected for two-year terms in even-numbered years, and the vice-president and treasurer are elected for two-year terms in odd-numbered years. The president, as a full-time, paid employee, may not serve as a member of a settlement council, but other members of the executive council may do so. Competition, especially for the position of president, is intense, with the requirement of an absolute majority forcing some settlement representatives into uncomfortable compromises. Any member of the executive council can be removed from office by an "extraordinary resolution," which can be passed only by three-quarters of the directors present and voting. In the event of a vacancy in the executive council, the board of directors designates a replacement to serve until the next annual general meeting.

Meetings of the Board of Directors

The bylaws of the FMSA require that a meeting of the board of directors be held at least once every three months, and provide that the president may, with sufficient notice, call such additional meetings as are deemed necessary. There are also provisions enabling members of the board to require the president to call special meetings. These provisions no longer have great practical importance, since custom and the weight of business dictate monthly meetings. At any meeting five voting members constitute a quorum. Members of the executive council cannot vote at FMSA meetings, except that the president of the FMSA may cast the deciding vote in case of a tie.

Meetings are usually held at the FMSA's office in Edmonton. They take place on weekends, extending from 8:30 A.M. to 4:30 P.M. on Saturdays and from 9:00 A.M. until noon on Sundays. In addition to the twelve members of the board of directors, other people—such as members of the FMSA staff, its lawyer, and invited government officials—usually attend the meetings (with permission, the author attended a considerable number of meetings as an observer). Board meetings follow a conventional format.

Major and Minor Items

Matters that concern all or most of the settlements usually find a place on the agenda of board meetings. Some of these matters are clearly of major importance in that they have profound implications for the well-being of the settlements. The matters deemed most important appear on the agenda of virtually every meeting. For example, the related matters of protecting the settlements' land and the litigation concerning subsurface resources take up, in one way or another, at least an hour of a typical meeting. Both the president and the FMSA's lawyer may be directed to address a matter regarding surface rights compensation from oil companies working on settlement lands; correspondence from the law firm handling the suit against the government may be discussed at some length; and the FMSA's team of negotiators concerning a new act to govern the settlements may be asked for a progress report.

It would be a mistake to suppose that the FMSA board deals only with matters of great consequence. A good deal of time at each meeting is taken up by routine matters, such as authorizing expenditures of a housekeeping nature, directing the president to write letters of thanks, approving the wording of applications for government grants and submissions, and so on.

Controversial and Uncontroversial Items

It should be emphasized that important matters are not necessarily controversial, nor are unimportant ones uncontroversial. Indeed, the matters regarded as most important by board members are least likely to generate heated debate. In particular, consensus in regard to protection of the land base is so broad and deep that "issues" relating to this matter are confined to questions of tactics rather than strategy or principle, and are addressed by the board in a spirit of cooperation, with an emphasis on reaching consensus rather than airing disagreements.

This is not to say that board meetings have more the character of the academic seminar than the political forum. On the contrary, most meetings include several heated debates. The type of proposal most likely to provoke combat is one that is seen as undermining the autonomy of one or more settlements. For example, at one meeting several board members expressed concern that certain settlement councils were "free-lancing" in their efforts to acquire housing for their constituents. Opponents of this practice raised two issues of equity, both relating to the differences among settlement councils in skill, diligence and/or luck in persuading government officials of the severity of their need for housing. The first issue was the claim that gains for one settlement could, and often did, cause shortages for others. The second was the claim that gains for the settlements could and did lead to hardship for poverty-stricken Metis not living on the settlements. When the debate became heated, it was decided that facts and figures should be collected by the president and staff and that the matter of housing should be discussed at a later meeting.

Internal and External Items

Internal matters are those which deal almost exclusively with settlement or FMSA matters, and which can be handled by the FMSA without the authorization of any governmental or nongovernmental agency. External matters are those that involve significant conflict, cooperation or negotiation with any such agency.

The most important generalization that can be made about board meetings in regard to this internal/external dimension is that the agenda of the typical meeting is concerned overwhelmingly with external rather than internal matters. In a typical meeting, that of January 1984, only eight internal items were discussed, while sixteen external items were on the agenda, including such diverse subjects as the provisions of the provincial government's proposed new Child Welfare Act, amendments to be made to the procedures for electing members of the FMSA's executive council, and applications to the federal Department of the Secretary of State for funding to prepare Cree instructional materials.

Central Features of Board Meetings

One feature of the board's work that is quite evident is the wide range of matters with which it deals. At one meeting, the board dealt with matters as diverse as Cree language retention, settlement housing, and the future constitutional status of the Metis. As well, the board deals with a wide variety of agencies. In addition to its internal operations and its relationships with the MDB, agenda items described above concerned the federal Department of the Secretary of State, the Alberta Department of Housing, and two provincial government committees, among others. Third, it is obvious by direct implication that an effective board member has to have a considerable familiarity with provincial and federal laws, programs and policies, that he/she must be well acquainted with the structure and functioning of the Alberta government, must possess the political acumen to recognize channels of influence within it, and must do a good deal of supplementary work in order to make useful contributions at board meetings. Fourth, it is evident that a number of matters that would seem to fall within the purview of the MDB are in fact decided by more senior government officials. In particular, it is clear that the ADM to whom the MDB reports occupies a crucial role in relation to the FMSA and the settlements. Finally, it is evident that the president plays a pivotal role in the FMSA. Almost every item on the agenda of the January 1984 meeting mentioned above involved the president, either by way of actions already taken by him, activities in which he was currently involved, or instructions to him by the board to initiate new actions.

Two general observations about the actual working of the FMSA can be made at this point. First, in spite of the central role of the president mentioned above, the FMSA is just that—a *federation*. It represents the settlements, it does not govern them. This feature of the FMSA reveals itself in two ways. In the first place, the autonomy of the individual settlements is firmly respected in dealing as they desire with matters not seen as relevant to all settlements. Only rarely does this require a warning to the FMSA to "back off." Usually the FMSA adheres to a tacit understanding that certain settlement policies, priorities and decisions are none of its concern; for example, the FMSA would not question the decision of a settlement to opt for the construction of a short stretch of paved road in preference to a longer stretch of gravel road. In the second place, the FMSA president must exercise discretion when expressing the views of the FMSA. On the one hand, he is lauded for creatively pursuing the FMSA's objectives, especially those that have been stated explicitly at board meetings. On the other hand, however, if he is seen to go too far in interpreting the wishes of the FMSA without adequate consultation or authorization, he is gently but firmly reminded that his conduct is unacceptable. Repeated arrogations of authority are certain to result in humbling rebukes at a board meeting.

The other general point that can be made about the actual working of the FMSA is that in it, inevitably, influence is distributed unequally. During the period in which the author observed meetings, there was a considerable turnover of personnel. Four of the eight council chairmen were replaced, as were all members of the executive council except the treasurer. On the basis of this "eyeball empiricism," it was determined that the following characteristics were the most conducive to acquiring and exercising greater influence in the FMSA:

> *Occupying the position of president.* Of course there can be (and have been) comparatively weak FMSA presidents. However, the operative word here is "comparatively." Council members take great care in choosing a president. Other things being equal, they would prefer to vote for a close friend rather than an acquaintance, a person from their own settlement rather than another, a person from their own region (that is, east or west) rather than the other. However, it is rarely the case that other things are equal, and the councillors are well aware of the crucial role played by the president both within their own organization and their relationship to other agencies. Accordingly, they have every reason to select a president who has the skills and aptitudes to do the job well, even if that requires voting contrary to a "sectarian" preference. Thus, one reason why the

president tends to be highly influential is that he/she is certain to be a person of exceptional ability. Another reason for the great influence of the president is that the position is full-time. Naturally, the incumbent acquires knowledge and information unavailable to other board members. In particular, through constant contact with government officials the president develops a finesse in dealing with politicians and civil servants that cannot be matched by other board members.

Forthrightness. Any hint of indecision is held in very low esteem by Metis politicians. This is not to say that in order to be influential a board member must be aggressive and outspoken. On the contrary, undue combativeness is seen as a fault. The point is that those who take an unequivocal position on important issues are admired, and those who are admired are more influential than those who are not.

Experience. For obvious reasons, those who have served on the board for a considerable length of time are looked to by others for guidance.

Intelligence. With each passing year, the issues faced by the FMSA become more complex and more decisive for the future, the pitfalls become deeper, and the cost of poor judgement higher. Board members with the acuteness to grasp complexities and foresee dangers are becoming increasingly influential.

Diligence. Board members who "do their homework" and come to meetings well prepared are far more influential than those who try to "play it by ear."

Dedication. The main interest of some board members is seen to be that of safeguarding the interests, as they see them, of their own settlements. The most influential members are those who are seen as deeply committed to the common good of all the settlements.

Moral probity. Board members do not pretend to be saintly, but almost all quietly subscribe to the Christian virtues. Honesty, fidelity and humility appear to be especially esteemed, and any board member who is seen to possess these qualities in unusual measure carries great weight with the others.

During the period when these observations were being made, four very different board members seemed to be exceptionally influential. Most influential by far was the president, Albert Chartier.[4] A native of the northernmost of the settlements, Chartier was one of the few members of any of the settlements who possessed a university degree. However, his influence did not derive from academic education alone. He had been a member, and the chairman, of his own settlement council, and therefore had a good deal of political experience both at the settlement level and at the level of the FMSA. As well, he was an active member of the Progressive Conservative party. One of his great strengths was his skill and resourcefulness in cultivating a wide range of contacts with both politicians and bureaucrats. Consequently, his understanding of political processes, especially those dominated by white officials, was unrivalled by his associates, and he had enormous influence on his associates during the difficult negotiations with the provincial government on matters that would profoundly affect the future status of the settlements.

Another influential board member was the treasurer, Ernest Williams. The basis of Williams's influence was quite different from Chartier's. For one thing, it did not derive from his position on the executive council. For another, Williams was about twenty years older than Chartier. Finally, Williams was not as effective an orator as Chartier. Williams's influence derived principally from his long experience, his dedication to the well-being of the settlements, and his moral probity. Williams seldom spoke, either during the meetings or in the informal discussions surrounding them, but when he spoke he was heeded. In fact, he seemed to exercise a sort of informal veto power; when Williams expressed doubts about a proposed course of action, the matter was pursued only after further careful study.

The third influential member of the board was Ronny Fraser, chairman of the council of one of the eastern settlements. The basis of Fraser's influence was similar to that of Williams, although Fraser was much younger. He was highly regarded for his experience, dedication and moral probity, but his influence was further enhanced by two additional characteristics. First, he was very forthright, a trait much admired by Metis politicians. Second, Fraser's council was generally recognized by board members as one of the best organized, most dedicated and most innovative of all. He was given a good deal of credit for this performance, which enhanced his standing in the FMSA.

The final influential member of the board, Ricky Maskwa, differed strikingly from the others. A young chairman of one of the eastern settlements, Maskwa was the most outspoken member of the board. A man of exceptional intelligence and political acumen, he was well informed about matters concerning the FMSA, and when in doubt about the advisability of proposed policies, tenaciously questioned their proponents. Although the president was often the object of Maskwa's searching questions, strong bonds of mutual respect grew between these two able and vigorous men. Maskwa was selected to serve with the president on the Joint Metis-Government Committee. Maskwa was eventually elected president of the FMSA.

Council Members' Assessments of the FMSA

In the last chapter, interviews with thirty-three of the forty chairmen of the settlement councils were discussed. Unreported there were responses to certain questions regarding the FMSA. The first question asked was: "Do you think the FMSA is helpful to your settlement?" The responses are summarized in Table 8.

Table 8
Helpfulness of FMSA to Metis Settlements

Response	Number	Percentage
Yes	26	78.8
Qualified yes	5	15.2
No	1	3.0
Don't know/no answer	1	3.0
Total	33	100.0

The second question was: "What good does it do?" Councillors were encouraged to give more than one answer to this question if they chose, and most did so. Twenty-nine of the thirty-one councillors who found the FMSA helpful gave reasons for their evaluation. Of the twenty-nine, at least twenty (about 70 percent) gave one or more of the following reasons: 1) activities in support of securing the settlement land base, including its leading role in initiating the litigation over subsurface rights; 2) lobbying governments for financing and programs; 3) devising and acting as a clearing-house for ideas and initiatives worthwhile to the settlements; 4) promoting unity among the settlements on matters of common concern; 5) effectively and successfully presenting the case for better and prompter payment of surface rights compensation; 6) devising and finding funds for programs to promote employment on the settlements; and 7) creating an agency, Settlement Sooniyaw, to promote systematic economic development on the settlements.

Table 9
Performance of FMSA President

Response	Number	Percentage
Good or excellent	18	54.5
Satisfactory	9	27.3
Poor	3	9.1
Don't know/no answer	3	9.1
Total	33	100.0

The third question asked was: "Is there anything about the FMSA that you do not like?" Fifty-one percent of the respondents gave a "yes" or "qualified yes" answer to this question. However, a majority of the respondents who found the FMSA inadequate could not identify a specific criticism. Moreover, only one shortcoming—the FMSA's failure to communicate effectively with the settlements—was mentioned by as many as four councillors. Only two other criticisms—that the FMSA did not allow the Settlement Sooniyaw sufficient autonomy, and that it infringed unduly on the independence of individual settlements—were noted by as many as three councillors. Evidently the FMSA is held in very high regard by the settlement councillors.

Finally, the councillors were asked: "Do you think the president of the FMSA has done a good job?" Respondents were then asked to explain their judgements. The responses to the general question are presented in Table 9. Thirty of the thirty-three councillors felt that the president's personal qualities and achievements, especially those that are most visible in the public arena, were highly advantageous to the FMSA and thereby the settlements. Mentioned in this context were his education, speaking ability, general polish, and political acumen. Several respondents remarked that these qualities filled them with pride and confidence. Other qualities and skills for which the president was commended were his adeptness in running meetings, his dedication to the well-being of the FMSA and the settlements, his industriousness, and his skill as a lobbyist. In a negative vein, four respondents felt that the president made too many decisions without consulting the board.

NOTES

1. Actually there are two complementary suits, one brought by a settlement on behalf of the settlements, and one a class action suit brought by an individual settler on behalf of all settlers.
2. Letter from the Honourable Marvin E. Moore, Minister of Municipal Affairs to Dr. Grant MacEwan, 2 April 1982; contained in Appendix 2 of the Report of the MacEwan Joint Metis-Government Committee to Review the Metis Betterment Act and Regulations.
3. In its application for incorporation as a society under the Societies Act, the federation stated the following as its objects:

    (a) To act as an agency for the co-operation of the Boards of the Settlement Associations formed pursuant to the provisions of the Metis Betterment Act and the regulations thereunder, (hereinafter referred to as the Associations), and to promote the advancement and betterment of the members of the Associations;

    (b) To co-ordinate the efforts of the Associations and to consider and deal with all matters and questions relating to the Associations and the members thereof;

    (c) To provide a medium for the expression of the views and suggestions of the Boards of the Associations on matters pertaining to the advancement and betterment of the members of the Associations and to unite members thereof in the bonds of mutual understanding;

(d) To render advice and assistance to the Boards of the Associations;

(e) To co-operate with the member of the Executive Council who is charged with the administration of the Metis Betterment Act;

(f) To secure united action for the improvement of legislation, regulations and governmental policies pertaining to the Associations and the members thereof;

(g) To hold conferences and meetings for the discussion and resolution of the needs and problems of the Associations and the members thereof;

(h) To promote the evolution of local or regional activities amongst the said Associations having regard to the indispensability of local effort, self-determination and self-government;

(i) To consider and discuss all questions affecting the interest of the Associations and the members thereof, and to initiate and promote delegations in relation to general matters affecting the Associations and the members thereof;

(j) To originate and promote improvements for the general welfare of the Associations and the members thereof, and to take such other steps and proceedings as may be deemed expedient in that behalf;

(k) To organize and develop comprehensive programs that are of relevance to the Associations and the members thereof;

(l) To stimulate interest in and appreciation of the needs and problems of the Metis population, and to promote the development of programs to meet the said needs and problems;

(m) To enter into any arrangements and agreements with any government, body corporate or authority that may seem conducive to the Society's objects or any of them and to obtain from such government, body corporate or authority any rights, privileges and concessions which the Society may think it desirable to obtain and to carry out, exercise and comply with any such arrangements and agreements, rights, privileges, and concessions;

(n) To sell, manage, lease, mortgage, dispose of, or otherwise deal with the property of the Society;

(o) To receive, and acquire by gift, bequest, devise, transfer or otherwise, property of every nature and description for the purposes of the Society;

(p) To subscribe to become a member of, and co-operate with other organizations, either incorporated or not, whose objects are altogether or in part similar to those of the Society;

(q) To purchase, take or lease or otherwise acquire any lands, buildings, or property, real and personal, which may be requisite for the purpose of or capable of being conveniently used in connection with the objects of the Society;

(r) To invest and deal with such moneys of the Society as are not immediately required, in such manner as may from time to time be determined;

(s) To do all such other things as are incidental or conducive to the attainment of the objects and the exercise of the powers of the Society.

4. It should be kept in mind that pseudonyms are used throughout this study.

6

The Metis Development Branch

For many years no branch of the provincial government had specific responsibility for the Metis settlements. Jurisdiction over the settlements was assigned to a section of the Bureau of Relief of the Department of Social Services and Community Health. With the onset of the Depression, this section was given responsibility for the relocation of people on relief in Alberta cities and towns to rural areas, where it was hoped they could make their living from the soil. After the passage of the Metis Population Betterment Act, this section of the Bureau of Relief was also given responsibility for the relocation of Metis who wished to move onto the settlements.[1]

In the mid-1940s the Metis Rehabilitation Branch, still within the Department of Social Services and Community Health, was created. It was a distinct agency with responsibility for the settlements. The branch was in a paternal relationship to the settlements, a relationship reflected in the scope of its activities on the settlements:

> During this period, the Metis Rehabilitation Branch provided practically all services to the Settlement Areas—operation of schools and involvement in secondary and adult education, construction and maintenance of roads, stores, agriculture and ranching activities, control of timber (including fire-fighting), trapping, hunting and fishing, many aspects of policing services, house construction, power lines and house wiring, issuing assistance, child abuse and care, registrar of births and deaths, issuing of marriage licences, emergency ambulance services, counselling, and in many instances the Area Supervisor had to act in the capacity of a midwife.[2]

The Metis Rehabilitation Branch was also influential in settlement government. Earlier in this period a three-person council, with its own chairman, was elected in each settlement, But a supervisor or manager, an employee of the branch, was stationed in each settlement and his judgement was decisive on all important matters. As a matter of administrative practice, he was the only contact between the settlers (including council members) and the government. And as a matter of self-interest, he was in a position to provide significant benefits to those who complied with his wishes and to withhold them from dissidents. Settlers who recalled those days agreed that the councils had no effective powers. Later, the councils were changed to five-person bodies in which two members were elected, two were appointed by the minister, and the area supervisor was chairman *ex officio*. Knowledgeable observers judge that this seemingly significant change meant little since the dominant position of the supervisor was already well established.

In 1980 the Metis Rehabilitation Branch underwent an important symbolic and practical change. It was moved from the Department of Social Services to the Department of Municipal Affairs, and its name was changed to the MDB. Repeatedly requested by the FMSA, this change entailed a rejection of the view that the creation and maintenance of the settlements was simply a social welfare scheme, in favour of the view that they were more than anything else a form of local government. The branch was placed under the authority of the ADM in charge of Improvement Districts, and the new director of the MDB, unlike his predecessors, was a specialist in economic development rather than social work.

In 1986 the position of the MDB was altered by a reorganization of the Improvement Districts Division. The MDB, renamed the Metis Settlement Branch (MSB), is one of the three branches (the others are Special Services Branch and Metis Services Branch) which compose the Native Services Unit. Each of these branches reports directly to the ADM. The MSB is the only agency of the provincial government that is concerned exclusively with the settlements, and it is likely to retain that status for some time to come. Nevertheless, from the standpoint of function, the MSB is not simply the successor of the MDB. The energies of the MSB are concentrated on two major (and interrelated) transitions. First, the MSB is facilitating the development of more direct relationships between the settlements and regular departments of the provincial government, in the manner of ordinary municipalities. Second, it is assisting the settlements in developing the personnel and the practices which will enable them to play a much larger role in managing their own affairs. Because the MSB is concentrating so heavily on transitional measures, it is difficult to portray accurately the current relationship between "the branch" and the settlements, much less forecast future relationships. Accordingly, risking the possibility that it will turn out to be primarily a matter of historical interest, the following discussion concentrates on the 1980-86 period.

Organization of the MDB

The senior official of the MDB is its director. Little about the specific responsibilities of the director can be learned from the official job description, which indicates little more than that he bears primary responsibility for maintaining and improving the services provided by the branch to the settlements, while doing his best to please his superiors within the department, other government agencies, the FMSA, and other Native organizations.

The staff of the MDB consists of employees in the central office in Edmonton and in the regional offices in High Prairie and St. Paul. In addition to the director, seven staff members are located in Edmonton. Three managers are the senior members of this staff. The first, the manager of planning and project development, is responsible for devising programs and projects in the realm of economic development and land use, and also in the area of local government, designed to enhance the well-being of the settlements. He is also responsible for the day-to-day legal transactions in which the MDB is involved, especially those which require contractual engagements with oil and gas companies. The manager of training and communications is responsible for the planning, initiation and implementation of training and educational programs on the Metis settlements, as well as being the focus through which the MDB regularly communicates with settlement councils and settlers. The manager of operations provides general management for the operations side of the MDB to ensure effective control of activities and the delivery of services to the settlements. This is achieved through the direction of two district managers and a central office staff. Budgeting, contract administration, expenditure approval, five-year plans, building inspections and the implementation and control of various systems and procedures are part of this manager's responsibilities. Also employed at the central office are an administrative officer and an oil and gas coordinator, whose responsibilities are mainly of a clerical nature in regard to oil, gas and seismic activities on the settlements. The other two employees at the central office do secretarial and clerical work.

Each district office is headed by a district manager, seconded by an assistant district manager. Also employed at each district office is a maintenance worker, who looks after public works on the settlements, and a secretary-receptionist. An employee of the MDB is also stationed at the northernmost settlement which, although counted as a western settlement, is too far from High Prairie to be serviced from there.

The principal task of the district offices is now to provide information, advice and other services to the settlements from a location near at hand, thereby significantly reducing the delay and inconvenience of routing all business through the Edmonton office. Above all, it was intended that decentralization of authority to the district offices would significantly accelerate the approval of projects and expenditures proposed by the settlement councils. Unfortunately, this intention has not been fulfilled. In particular, the hoped-for acceleration of the approval of expenditures has not materialized.

Finances

There are profound interrelationships between the economic and the political dimensions of life. Economics is sometimes described as pertaining to the allocation of scarce resources, but scarce resources are also allocated by political practices, procedures and institutions. This interrelationship between the economic and the political is clearly discernible in the experience of the Alberta Metis settlements. For example, the dispute over the ownership of subsurface resources on the settlements is not a purely legal matter, it is clearly also a political and economic issue. In Chapter 4 it was seen that the political issue commonly identified as the most difficult by settlement councillors is the allocation of scarce resources to the members of their settlements.

A large proportion of the revenues of the settlements is provided by senior governments, especially the provincial government, and the largest proportion of provincial government funds is channelled through the budget of the MDB. Whatever the motives of settlement politicians, it is evident that the greater the amount of funds they can extract from government, the better their purposes will be achieved.

Although there is a considerable conjunction of interests between the Metis politicians and officials of the MDB, there are nevertheless some inherent bases of conflict. While the Metis politicians are aware that the budget of the MDB is finite, they naturally see their needs as exceptionally pressing and hold the MDB responsible for being insufficiently energetic in seeking budget increases. As well, MDB officials are concerned with strict financial accountability. While Metis politicians accept the principle of accountability, they tend to see some of the specific requirements as intrusive, requiring accounting that is too detailed to serve reasonable purposes. Finally, there are regular disagreements as to the most appropriate means of making use of the MDB's budget. On the one hand, the settlements occasionally propose programs and projects that the MDB sees as inappropriate for a variety of reasons: excessive cost, lack of long-term benefits, inadequate levels of expertise, and so on. On the other hand, the MDB sometimes proposes—and sometimes implements without adequate consultation—programs and projects which the settlement councillors and the FMSA feel have little relation to the abilities, needs and aspirations of the settlers. However, before venturing any further generalizations about the political implications of financing, it would be appropriate to provide some specific information about the revenues and expenditures of the MDB, the settlements, and the FMSA.

In 1962-63, the budget of the MDB was less than $250,000, by 1969-70 it was over $900,000, and since the MDB has been relocated to the Department of Municipal Affairs its annual budget has been increased to approximately $3 million. Before considering the budget of the MDB more fully, it would be helpful to gain some understanding of the budgets of the settlements themselves. The operational revenues of the settlements are obtained from provincial appropriations (the "vote budget") and the Metis Settlement Trust Fund (the "trust budget"). Both the vote budget and the trust budget are received initially as lump sums. However, by long-standing agreement both budgets are allocated among the settlements such that 70 percent is divided evenly and 30 percent on a per capita basis. Beginning in 1986, there was a considerable change in the financing of the settlements by the branch. Financing in the 1984-85 fiscal year provides a backdrop for describing subsequent developments. The 1984-85 vote budget, which is presented in Table 10, illustrates this distribution.[3]

Table 10
Vote Budget, 1984-1985

Settlement	70% Even	30% Per capita	% Population	Budget
Highgrass Plain	$96,250	$61,050	18.5	$157,300
Pickerel Lake	96,250	27,060	8.2	123,310
Jackpine	96,250	42,570	12.9	138,820
Paskwaw	96,250	28,380	8.6	124,630
Osprey Lake	96,250	55,440	16.8	151,690
Aspen River	96,250	47,190	14.3	143,440
Green Prairie	96,250	34,320	10.4	130,570
Viscount	96,250	33,990	10.3	130,240
Total	$770,000	$330,000	100.0	$1,100,000

The similar distribution but smaller size of the trust budget for 1984-85 is exhibited in Table 11. It should be noted that the total trust budget was not $389,400 but $462,000; the remaining $72,600 was committed to the financing of the FMSA.

Table 11
Trust Budget, 1984-1985

Settlement	70% Even	30% Per capita	% Population	Budget
Highgrass Plain	$34,072	$21,612	18.5	$55,684
Pickerel Lake	34,072	9,580	8.2	43,652
Jackpine	34,072	15,070	12.9	49,142
Paskwaw	34,072	10,047	8.6	44,119
Osprey Lake	34,072	19,626	16.8	53,698
Aspen River	34,072	16,706	14.3	50,778
Green Prairie	34,072	12,150	10.4	46,222
Viscount	34,072	12,033	10.3	46,105
Total	$272,576	$116,824	100.0	$389,400

Expenditures from both budgets must be approved by the department. In the case of large expenditures this can involve the ADM, the deputy minister, or even the minister. Ordinarily, however, authorization of expenditures is handled by the MDB. The vote and trust budgets are used for somewhat different purposes. Generally speaking, the trust budget is used for more discretionary purposes, while the vote budget is used for purposes deemed essential to the welfare of the settlements.

The financial contribution of the MDB to the settlements has always been considerably greater than has been revealed so far. For example, for several years the MDB has been paying for the installation of water and sewage facilities on the settlements. In 1984, an official of the MDB estimated that the eventual cost of this endeavour would be approximately $12 million. The MDB has financed a number of training programs—for settlement administrators and for apprentice carpenters, for example—as well as seminars on financial accountability. The MDB also makes an annual contribution to the core budget of the FMSA. The 1984-85 core budget of the FMSA is presented in Table 12.

Table 12
Budget of the FMSA, 1984-1985

Source	Amount ($)
Metis Betterment Trust Fund	73,920
Secretary of State	37,061
Municipal Affairs	30,000
Carpentry Training Program	15,145
Settlement Sooniyaw Corporation	1,683
Total	157,809

After 1984-85, part of the funding of the settlements and the FMSA continued to come in the form of vote and trust appropriations. However, there were no major increases in these allocations—for the most part, they simply kept pace with inflation. In fact, the financial contribution to the settlements increased markedly after 1985. After the replacement of the MDB by the MSB, the branch began to make sizeable special purpose grants to the settlements with a view to enhancing their ability to assume a significantly larger role in managing their own affairs. By 1989-90 these grants amounted to just under $1 million per year. Considering that during this period the provincial government was committed to, and was to a considerable extent practising, a policy of fiscal restraint, it certainly cannot be said that the government was paying mere lip service to Metis betterment in the financial realm.

Facts and figures, especially concerning the crucial realm of finance, are a requisite to understanding the relationships between the MDB, the settlements and the FMSA. However, quantitative data only reveal possibilities for conflict and cooperation, they provide little insight into either the tone or the substance of the relationships which are of interest, and which will now be considered. First the views of the settlement councillors and officers of the FMSA concerning the MDB will be examined.

Metis Views of the MDB

During the interviews of settlement councillors, certain questions were asked about the MDB. The first question was: "What do you think of the MDB?" There were both negative and positive responses. For example, one council chairman described MDB officials as "a bunch of red-necked sons of bitches . . . I have more faith in my five-year-old daughter than the MDB has in elected Metis councillors." Another remarked that "it's too bad that we don't have more snipers." At the other extreme, one council chairman described MDB officials as "always cooperative, helpful and courteous." Another praised the competence and dedication of the MDB staff, attributing all dissatisfaction to the conduct of governmental officials senior to the MDB, and criticized a number of his associates for adopting an unduly combative stance towards members of the MDB. The most common response, however, was more balanced, identifying both strengths and weaknesses of the MDB.

Most settlement councillors and FMSA officers interviewed felt the strengths of the MDB were almost entirely attributable to the merits of individual MDB employees, rather than merits of policies, programs or practices. In particular, most saw the MDB staff, especially the top managers in the central office and the then director, as highly competent and eager to do their best for the settlements. The view was widespread that shortcomings in the performance of the MDB were largely attributable to obstructions imposed by senior officials in the Department of Municipal Affairs and by representatives of the attorney general concerned about the litigation between the settlements and the provincial government. Several of the councillors regretted what they saw as the stifling of the MDB's "good, young staff."

Many of the negative comments about the MDB also related to members of the staff. This may seem contradictory, but in fact it is easy to explain. At the time the interviews were conducted, most of the councillors were impressed by the ability and dedication of the staff of the MDB's central office, especially the director and a young manager. However, they saw these men as atypical, and not what they could expect in the future. Their suspicions that the MDB was an inhospitable environment for people intent on doing a good job were confirmed when the director and two young managers resigned. Several respondents held that the MDB should be first and foremost a clientele agency, acting as an advocate within government for the settlements in the same way that the Department of Agriculture commonly pleads the case of farmers. The view was widely shared that the MDB spent too much time and energy attempting to control activities on the settlements and too little attempting to facilitate their economic and political development.

Closely connected to the foregoing criticism was the recurrent charge of paternalism based on ignorance. Two kinds of ignorance were commonly attributed to the MDB. The first was ignorance of "the Metis outlook." For example, a number of respondents said that most officials of the MDB never understood that uncultivated land was regarded by the Metis not as "wasteland" but as an indispensable habitat for hunting, trapping and gathering. One respondent, who was generally favourably disposed towards the MDB, noted that "the MDB sometimes seems to forget that we're only half white." The other type of ignorance, less closely linked to cultural differences, was attributed to the fact that the senior officials of the MDB were deskbound in Edmonton and therefore not sufficiently familiar with the needs, aspirations and prospects of the settlements. The principal MDB officials, according to a number of councillors, had a weak grasp of local problems common to all the settlements and even less awareness of the differences among the settlements.

During the period when the interviews were conducted, the expression of paternalism most galling to the councillors was the decision of the MDB to spend several million dollars over several years installing water and sewage treatment facilities on the settlements, without consulting the settlement councils about the advisability of such a large expenditure on this as opposed to other projects. Not surprisingly, councillors who opposed this project were especially vehement in their condemnation of the MDB. But the heat of their condemnation was no greater than that of a councillor who strongly favoured the program. While forcefully asserting his opinion that in the current state of the environment "purified running water is not a luxury but a hygienic necessity," he strongly censured the MDB for proceeding without consultation.

Councillors forcefully criticized the MDB for two reasons familiar to civil servants. First, the councillors maintained that there were excessive delays in approving or disapproving proposals made by the settlements; it should be emphasized that blame for the delays was not ascribed exclusively to the MDB. Part of the problem, according to the councillors, was that senior officials in the Department of Municipal Affairs, as well as agents of the attorney general, often lengthened the delays by a time-consuming scrutiny of proposals. Nevertheless, most of the blame was attributed to the MDB itself, which was held to be deliberate to the point of obstructiveness in its evaluation of proposals. Second, the MDB was held to be uninformative to the point of secrecy in its dealings with the councils and the FMSA. Several councillors saw this as related to the MDB's paternalistic attitude towards the settlements. In their view, the MDB had its own agenda for expenditure of the part of its budget not committed to other purposes, and preferred not to consult with the Metis.

The second question which the councillors were asked was: "Do you think the MDB has been improving or getting worse in recent years?" Thirty of the thirty-three councillors interviewed responded to this question. Interestingly, fifteen of these said that the MDB was improving, while only seven said that it was getting worse; the remaining eight saw no significant change. How could councillors see the MDB as improving while being negative about its performance? Two considerations which emerged in the interviews account for this apparent disparity. First, at the time when the interviews were conducted the councillors were impressed by the ability and diligence of the MDB director and one of the young managers. Although these men had already given notice of resignation, their performance clearly influenced the councillors. Second, it became evident in the course of the interviews that many of the councillors were not comparing the performance of the MDB at the time of the interview with its performance at an earlier time. Instead, they were comparing the MDB with the Metis Rehabilitation Branch in the Department of Social Services. While they had plenty of criticisms of the MDB, not surprisingly most of them found it markedly preferable to deal with an agency with a significantly increased budget and an orientation towards political and economic development rather than social work.

The final question regarding the MDB was: "Is the district office of the MDB helpful to you?" Favourable responses regarding the district offices tended to be given by the less experienced councillors. All favourable responses commended the district offices as sources of information and advice, which was found particularly helpful by newer council members. The unfavourable responses, with few exceptions, came from the more experienced councillors and focussed on matters relating to the processing of proposals, the delivery of services, and the settlement of grievances. These councillors had little to say about the competence and dedication of the staffs of the district offices. In their view, problems arose not from the personnel of these offices but from the system of which they were a part. Specifically, they complained that the district offices were so lacking in authority that they served only as an additional hurdle to leap before results could be obtained. They found that since all important matters had to be dealt with in Edmonton, routing them through the district offices served no other purpose than delay.

The MDB, then, was not held in high esteem by the settlement councillors. Although some members of the MDB's staff were well regarded, the councillors felt that its organization, policies, practices and institutional orientation left a great deal to be desired. At this juncture it is worth seeing if these negative sentiments were reciprocated by the MDB.

MDB Views of the Metis

The following observations are based on two types of evidence. First, in the 1983-85 period most of the nonclerical staff of the MDB were interviewed, including personnel in one of the district offices and in some cases consecutive incumbents of the same position. Second, during the same period the author attended a number of meetings of the board of directors of the FMSA and all-council meetings at which officials of the MDB made presentations, usually followed by question-and-answer sessions.

All the MDB officials interviewed believed that the quality of settlement government and politics had improved remarkably, in every important respect, during the preceding decade. All the members of the

MDB with whom the author spoke agreed that the general level of competence of the members of the settlement councils had improved strikingly in the preceding decade. The MDB members were not averse to taking some credit for this improvement, but they attributed much of the improvement to the fact that the Metis settlers were acquiring more and better formal education. MDB officials saw the greatly increased ability and propensity to take into account the short- and long-term effects of programs, policies and practices as the most dramatic of the improvements in the Metis leaders. The political improvements on the settlements were not seen by MDB officials as confined to the existing leadership group, however. Several of them remarked that there was a corresponding improvement in the competence and the public spirit of the "ordinary" settlers, especially on the more "progressive" settlements, as seen in the increased turnout and greater frequency of close contests in settlement elections. MDB officials also pointed to the development of the FMSA into an effective coordinating and lobbying organization as a sign of increased Metis political sophistication. In a more concrete vein, several MDB officials noted that both the settlement councils and the FMSA were becoming increasingly effective in securing and administering grants for both political and employment-generating purposes from agencies other than the MDB.

Not surprisingly, praise by MDB members was also mixed with criticism. Such criticism can be grouped into two categories, dealing with the relationships between the Metis politicians and their constituents, and with the relationships between the Metis politicians and the MDB.

Criticism of the relationships between politicians and their constituents was based on the charge of favouritism. Politicians were accused of pursuing disproportionately the interests of people like themselves, devoting most of their energies to objectives favoured by wage labourers, farmers and ranchers, while paying relatively little attention to those of their constituents who were more "traditional" in their outlooks and activities. The latter, partly because they tended to be politically inarticulate, for the most part were neglected. As well, it was maintained that there was a pattern in which many council members use their office to favour relatives and, to a lesser extent, friends. Houses, major house repairs, wells and jobs were among the services said to be allocated to relatives and friends of councillors, regardless of need. It should be noted that MDB members who identified this type of favouritism all emphasized that it is now less serious on most settlements than it was in the past.

MDB members voiced three main complaints about the Metis politicians' relationships with the MDB itself. First, they held that neither the settlement councils nor the FMSA were sufficiently sensitive to the constraints imposed on the MDB by law and by government policy. In the view of MDB officials, the Metis were too ready to condemn the MDB for its slow response to requests for approval of projects, and requirements that meticulous financial records be kept, when these difficulties arose not from the policies of the MDB but from legal requirements or from the need of the MDB to consult with other government agencies. Second, MDB officials were persuaded that the settlements did too little to enhance their financial independence and relied too heavily on the MDB and other government agencies. MDB members maintained that the settlement councils were lax even in ensuring that they collected the annual levies, and made little effort to expand their revenue base within the settlements. This reluctance was especially disturbing in light of the expressed desire of most of the Metis leaders to achieve a greater level of political autonomy for the settlements. MDB members maintained that government funds *always* come with strings attached, and that increased self-government by the Metis depended on increased self-taxation. This matter continues to cause considerable friction between Metis leaders and the MDB, frequently surfacing in discussions of the honoraria paid to councillors. By law, the secretary and each member of council is entitled to an honorarium of three dollars for each monthly council meeting. In practice, councillors receive monthly honoraria of one hundred dollars and council chairmen two hundred dollars. In addition, councillors receive an honorarium for each off-settlement meeting attended. Councillors complain that these payments are incommensurate with the time and energy they expend on their duties. Senior government officials have occasionally opposed this view by appealing to the literal meaning of "honorarium" as a token of appreciation for services rendered. Most MDB officials do not agree with this narrow definition, but they do hold that if the honoraria are increased, the added expense should be borne by the settlements as a step towards greater self-government. Finally, MDB officials complained that councillors often use the MDB as a scapegoat to deflect attention from their own shortcomings. In particular, it was felt that councillors often ignore information provided to them by the MDB, or procrastinate beyond deadlines and then accuse the MDB of having failed to provide the information at all.

Assessment and Implications

A good test of the fairness of praise or blame is whether those who receive it accept it as well founded. To the extent that this test is a good one, the officials of the MDB and the leaders of the Metis settlements seem to have taken each others' measure rather well, since some members of the MDB acknowledged the justice of a number of the Metis leaders' criticisms of their agency, while several Metis leaders acknowledged that some of the MDB criticisms were legitimate.[4]

The Metis leaders agreed with the MDB officials that the quality of government and politics on the settlements had improved dramatically in all respects during the preceding decade, and that this improvement was in large measure due to the fact that settlers were acquiring more and better formal education. This, they believed, had three important effects. First, it created a larger pool of potential settlement councillors. Second, it increased the willingness of settlers to elect better-educated councillors. Third, it helped to expand the "attentive public" on the settlements—the group of settlers who kept a close eye on the activities of their councillors and were unhesitant in offering either encouragement or dissent as they saw fit. Thus the councillors, like the MDB officials, saw political improvement not just in the leadership ranks but throughout the settlement populations. Again like the MDB officials, but more emphatically, Metis politicians saw the creation and increasing sophistication of the FMSA as a crucial factor in their political progress. Some of the more experienced Metis politicians agreed with the MDB's charge that it was sometimes used as a scapegoat to deflect attention from the councillors' own shortcomings. One council chairman, not an admirer of the MDB, remarked drolly that he found it most useful as a target to blame for some of his own shortcomings. Most councillors also acknowledged that there was some truth in the charge of favouritism. However, all maintained that it was declining rapidly and had practically disappeared on some settlements.

MDB officials concurred with much of the assessment of them by the Metis leaders. They agreed strongly with the judgement that the performance of the MDB had improved markedly when it was transferred from the Department of Social Services to the Department of Municipal Affairs. They shared the Metis view that this improvement had much to do with increased competence. However, they saw this competence less as a matter of absolute superiority of personnel than of greater fitness relative to the needs and aspirations of the settlements. That is, they saw their superiority as stemming from the greater appropriateness of an agency concerned mainly with political and economic development compared to one concerned mainly with social work.

MDB members also agreed that many of the defects attributed to the MDB by the Metis resulted from constraints imposed upon it, rather than from personal shortcomings or policies favoured by the MDB as a whole. For example, the slowness of MDB responses to proposals was attributed in large part to the constraints imposed by government financial regulations. The failure of the regional offices to measure up to expectations was also attributed to obstacles created outside the MDB. According to members of the MDB, senior officials both inside and outside the Department of Municipal Affairs had forbidden the devolution of authority that the MDB would have preferred, insisting that all but the most minor decisions be evaluated in Edmonton.

A similar response was made to the charge of paternalism. MDB officials acknowledged that, to some extent, the MDB was in a paternalistic relationship with the settlements. However, they maintained that this paternalism was an institutionalized constraint rather than an expression of the personal dispositions of members of the MDB. As was seen in Chapter 2, the councils of the Metis settlements do not even have the legal authority of a minor municipality. All the bylaws of the settlement councils must be ratified by the minister and, in accordance with the Metis Population Betterment Act, there are few official actions that can be taken by the councils without the authorization of the minister or the cabinet. Of necessity, the bulk of this authority is delegated to a bureaucratic agency, the MDB. Thus, an element of paternalism is built into the relationship between the MDB and the settlements, regardless of the wishes of either party, because as long as there is legislation that construes the settlement Metis as wards of the state, there must be an agency of the civil service which administers that wardship. This argument fails to counter the charge made by the Metis that the MDB's paternalism extends beyond the requirements of law, in that MDB members frequently fail to consult with the settlement councils and the FMSA before implementing major programs.

Some MDB officials agreed that MDB members located in Edmonton, who were the main decision makers in regard to the settlements, were often unfamiliar with the actual conditions on the settlements. However, they vehemently rejected the charges of some Metis leaders that MDB members knew next to nothing about problems faced by the settlements in general, and the diversity of the problems faced by different settlements in particular. It was recognized, however, that a considerable part of their time was consumed in paperwork, intragovernmental consultations and negotiations, and dealings with private enterprisers whose activities affected the well-being of the settlements. Furthermore, it was acknowledged that their contacts with the settlements were almost exclusively contacts with settlement leaders.[5]

If the Alberta Metis settlements are to acquire a significantly greater scope of political self-determination, tasks now performed by the MDB must be taken over by the settlements, the FMSA, other agencies established by the settlements for various purposes, or a combination of these. The most interesting implications of this examination of the MDB concern the possibility that the Metis could assume these tasks.

A number of considerations suggest that the Metis could perform tasks currently carried on by the MDB. Most of the MDB officials and most of the Metis leaders agree on the following points: 1) the pool of able Metis leaders and potential leaders is growing rapidly; 2) the level of comprehension of the workings of the provincial government has increased dramatically during the past decade, especially within the FMSA; 3) devolution of authority to the regional offices has not occurred; 4) Metis leaders are more familiar than members of the MDB with conditions that obtain generally on the settlements and also with the diversity of the settlements; and 5) the MDB adopts an unduly paternalistic stance towards the settlements. Therefore, to some extent, an enhanced level of political self-determination at the level of the settlements is possible. However, claiming that Metis *could* do work now done by the MDB is not equivalent to claiming that they *should* do so. It is possible that a Metis-dominated MDB (or a new agency performing similar tasks) would have all the shortcomings of the present MDB. For one thing, the favouritism that is acknowledged to persist on the settlements could become even more problematic if it infected the MDB as well as the councils. Moreover, it is possible that the creation of a Metis-dominated MDB would slow the movement towards a more meaningful transfer of authority from the provincial government to the settlements, in that the government might feel such a move would satisfy Metis aspirations to increased self-determination. Finally, the political attitudes, opinions, and aspirations of "ordinary" residents of the settlements have to this point been neglected. Accordingly, the next two chapters will examine several dimensions of the political orientations of the residents of the Metis settlements.

NOTES

1. MDB, *Metis Settlements in Alberta* (Edmonton: n.p., 1982), 10.
2. Ibid., 12.
3. Names of settlements, like names of persons, are pseudonyms.
4. It should be noted that these acknowledgements of the soundness of praise and blame occurred spontaneously in conversation. The author did not confront either side with the criticisms of the other.
5. A common complaint of Metis councillors is that the MDB's perceptions of their relationships with their constituents are unduly coloured by the complaints of a few malcontents who make regular visits to the regional offices.

7

External Political Orientations of the Metis Settlers

Attention in this study has so far been focussed on the governors rather than the governed. However, it takes little reflection to see that a study of a political organization which concentrates on the governors and ignores the governed is bound to be inadequate. A concern for accuracy, then, would be a sufficient reason for attending to the political orientations of "ordinary folks" as well as political leaders, but there is a further reason why attention to the governed as well as the governors is essential to the present study. One of the central interests of this book is in the *possibility* and *desirability* of increased political self-determination by the settlements, both of which are dependent upon the attitudes and opinions of the "ordinary" settlers. If the settlers, or a significant majority of them, are opposed to greater self-government, the case for it is severely undermined, if not destroyed. In particular, it is a requisite of increased self-government that most settlers have enough confidence in their current and prospective leaders that they are willing to see them invested with more authority. Accordingly, this chapter and the next are concerned with the political outlooks and activities of "ordinary" residents of the settlements.

Interviewing the Settlers

For a variety of reasons it was impossible to interview a reasonably representative sample of the residents of all eight settlements. The author thus chose to conduct interviews on two settlements: a large, eastern settlement, and a smaller, western one. Osprey Lake is an eastern settlement which is one of the largest of the eight. It occupies an area of about eighty thousand acres, and its population is around 720. It is divided by a paved provincial highway, although most of its area and population are on one side of the highway, so that most travel within the settlement is on gravel roads. The settlement land includes one lake and abuts another but there is no viable commercial fishery. Almost all of the land is rocky, a good deal of it swampy, and little of it fit for farming. Ranching, and in some cases associated growing of feed crops, is the most successful on-settlement source of income. A number of settlers work in various occupations in the nearest sizeable town, and some of the men leave the settlement for extended periods of seasonal employment, such as firefighting, construction and work in the oil fields, but the rate of unemployment and underemployment is very high.

Paskwaw is a western settlement which occupies about the same area as Osprey Lake but its population (around 350) is much smaller. It is located in an area of gently rolling bush and forest on both sides of the Elkhorn River. The nearest paved highway is fifteen miles away. A small town is located at the junction of the highway and the gravel road to the settlement, and from there it is a short trip to the major town in the area. Access to and within the settlement has been persistently impeded by poor transportation routes. The Elkhorn River is subject to flooding and for may years bridges were regularly washed away. Although the settlement was established in 1939, it was not until 1967 that a permanent bridge was completed. Roads within the settlement are still few and not very well constructed, and there is still no access to some of the settlement's more promising agricultural land. These problems of physical access have undoubtedly contributed to the settlement's relatively slow growth and small population. There are some successful farmers and ranchers in Paskwaw, in spite of the fact that agriculture is inhibited by mostly poor soil and transportation problems. Timber was overcut many years ago and, although a silvicultural program is now in place, forestry is not yet a practical proposition on the settlement. However, some settlers are employed full-time or part-time in lumber mills in the nearby towns. A number of settlers acquire seasonal employment in a variety of occupations, but unemployment and underemployment are consistently high.

Having decided to conduct interviews on these two settlements, the author formally requested permission from the board of the FMSA to do so, supplying written information about the nature and purposes of the study. Soon thereafter he was called on to appear at a board meeting to answer questions. It was made clear that permission would also be required from the settlement councils, since the FMSA did not have the authority to make such decisions on their behalf. After the author's oral presentation and a question period, the board approved the interview project. The chairman of the Osprey Lake settlement indicated that his settlement had already approved the request. He said that soon after the possibility of studying an eastern and a western settlement had been mooted, the settlement had held a general meeting at which it was decided that Osprey Lake should be studied. Moreover, he urged the author to "Do your damnedest to find fault with us; we want the nearest to the truth you can find." The response from Paskwaw was quite different and, initially, closer to what had been expected. They had not yet held a meeting but proposed to do so in the near future. The Paskwaw settlement council met later and rejected the proposal. However, soon thereafter the Paskwaw council invited the author to a general meeting of the settlement to state his case. After an oral presentation and close questioning, approval was given to undertake the study.

The selection of respondents was not scientific. Working from the most recent voters' list for a settlement council election, the author asked a school-aged settlement child to select a number at random from the total number of voters on the list. Taking the person designated by that number as the first interviewee, the author selected every sixth name thereafter from the Osprey Lake voters' list, which included about three hundred persons, and every fourth name from the Paskwaw voters' list, which contained about 175. When an individual would not, or could not, be interviewed, the name of the next person on the voters' list was substituted.

All the interviews were conducted by the author, who spent approximately three weeks at each settlement. The respondents were most hospitable and forthcoming, and the interviews rarely lasted less than half an hour. All but two of the interviews were private, the two exceptions being unilingual Cree speakers in which cases an interpreter was present. The anonymity of all participants in the study was guaranteed. Accordingly, in this chapter as throughout the book, not only the names of particular individuals but also the names of families, settlements, and landmarks are pseudonyms.

Although neither the size nor the method of selecting the samples would satisfy a scientific pollster, the responses nevertheless are representative of the adult populations of the two settlements. There was scarcely a household in either of the two communities in which no one was interviewed, and in several households more than one person was interviewed. Furthermore, the author had conversations with settlers who were not formally interviewed, and the range and intensity of their views closely paralleled those of the designated interviewees. More dubious than the reliability of the findings concerning the two settlements, however, are attempts to generalize these findings to the other six settlements. While it is acknowledged that there are many respects in which the eight settlements are similar, there are also important differences among them. Fortunately, two important differences were dealt with by virtue of the settlements chosen for study. First, it is sometimes held that there is a significant difference between the more populous and less populous settlements; Osprey Lake has a comparatively large population whereas Paskwaw's is comparatively small. Second, almost all observers find important differences between the eastern and western settlements; as noted earlier, Osprey Lake is located in the east, while Paskwaw is in the west.

Demographic Characteristics of the Respondents

At Osprey Lake, 54 percent (twenty-seven of fifty) of the respondents were male and 46 percent female. This compares with the voters' list ratio of 52 percent male and 48 percent female. At Paskwaw, 45.5 percent (twenty of forty-four) of the respondents were male and 54.5 percent female (compared to the voters' list ratio of 46 percent male and

Table 13
Age Distribution of Respondents

Osprey Lake			
Age	Number	Percentage	Cumulative Percentage
Under 21	4	8.0	8.0
21-24	5	10.0	18.0
25-29	10	20.0	38.0
30-34	1	2.0	40.0
35-39	5	10.0	50.0
40-44	8	16.0	66.0
45-49	4	8.0	74.0
50-54	3	6.0	80.0
55-59	3	6.0	86.0
60-64	3	6.0	92.0
Over 65	4	8.0	100.0
Total	50	100.0	100.0
Paskwaw			
Under 21	5	11.4	11.4
21-24	4	9.1	20.5
25-29	8	18.2	38.6
30-34	3	6.8	45.5
35-39	2	4.5	50.0
40-44	6	13.6	63.6
45-49	3	6.8	70.5
50-54	3	6.8	77.3
55-59	3	6.8	84.1
60-64	1	2.3	86.4
Over 65	6	13.6	100.0
Total	44	100.0	100.0

54 percent female). The age distributions of the respondents on the two settlements are displayed in Table 13. There is an unrepresentative shortage of respondents in the 30-34 age group and an excess in the 25-29 age group, but otherwise the sample appears to be reasonably representative. There is an important aspect in which the sample appears to be highly representative. It is generally agreed that on each settlement there are "leading families": four at Osprey Lake and three at Paskwaw. The proportions of these families interviewed and their proportions on the voters lists are very close, as Table 14 reveals.

Table 14
Leading Families: Interviewed and Actual

Osprey Lake		
Family	% Interviewed	% on Voters' List
Gregg	18.0	20.0
Allen	8.0	6.0
Bright	10.0	12.0
Cliche	8.0	6.0
Total	44.0	44.0
Paskwaw		
Miller	16.0	13.0
Chretien	6.0	7.0
Lapointe	16.0	14.0
Total	38.0	34.0

Respondents were asked how much formal education they had completed. Their replies are presented in Table 15. The "some secondary" category is very broad, ranging from a partial grade 7 to near-completion of grade 12, but a majority of the respondents in this category mentioned that they had attended high school. Typically those who entered grade 12 completed it, and it is noteworthy that a high school graduation rate of 20 percent is very high for a Native community.

There is evidence of a considerable difference between Osprey Lake and Paskwaw in levels of formal educational attainment. At the one extreme, only 8 percent of the respondents at Osprey Lake had not completed elementary school, while the corresponding figure for Paskwaw was 27 percent. At the other extreme, 20 percent of the respondents at Osprey Lake had completed high school, compared to only 7 percent at Paskwaw.

Table 15
Formal Education of Respondents

Osprey Lake		
Amount of Schooling	Number	Percentage
None	3	6.0
Some elementary	1	2.0
Completed elementary	4	8.0
Some secondary	29	58.0
Completed secondary	10	20.0
Some postsecondary	2	4.0
No answer	1	2.0
Total	50	100.0
Paskwaw		
None	5	11.4
Some elementary	7	15.9
Completed elementary	8	18.2
Some secondary	21	47.7
Completed secondary	3	6.8
Some postsecondary	0	0.0
Total	44	100.0

There was also a considerable difference between the two settlements in the respondents' ability to speak Cree, as shown in Table 16. In most cases, "some Cree" meant good, though imperfect, comprehension and fair to poor ability to speak. The striking thing about the Osprey Lake respondents is that almost half of them had no Cree at all; the situation is very different at Paskwaw.

Table 16
Competence in Cree of Respondents

Osprey Lake		
Level of Competence	Number	Percentage
No Cree	23	46.0
Some Cree	9	18.0
Fluent Cree	18	36.0
Total	50	100.0
Paskwaw		
No Cree	11	25.0
Some Cree	6	13.6
Fluent Cree	27	61.4
Total	44	100.0

At Osprey Lake, 78 percent of the respondents said that they belonged to a church or other religious organization, compared to 91 percent at Paskwaw. As Table 17 indicates, there is a striking difference in religious affiliation between the two settlements. In light of what is known of Metis history, especially in Alberta, the high proportion of Protestants comes as some surprise. The Protestants were almost equally divided between members of the United Church and members of a quite recently established Pentecostal church. Several informed observers warned against taking this high proportion of Protestant affiliation as typical of the eastern settlements. The strength of the United Church at Osprey Lake, they maintained, was largely the result of early patterns of missionary activity, while Protestant fundamentalism, though present in other settlements, is nowhere else as strong as at Osprey Lake. With its overwhelming preponderance of Roman Catholics, Paskwaw corresponds more closely to standard preconceptions about the religious convictions of Metis communities.

Table 17
Religious Affiliations of Respondents

Osprey Lake		
Religious Affiliation	Number	Percentage
Roman Catholic	20	40.0
Protestant	21	42.0
Non-denominational Christian	7	14.0
Native	0	0.0
No religion	1	2.0
No answer	1	2.0
Total	50	100.0
Paskwaw		
Roman Catholic	36	81.8
Protestant	3	6.8
Non-denominational Christian	3	6.8
Native	1	2.3
No answer	1	2.3
Total	44	100.0

Each respondent was asked how long he/she had lived on the settlement. The replies are presented in Table 18. Remarkable here, though not surprising, is the high proportion of long-term residents. Over 60 percent of the respondents had lived on the Osprey Lake settlement for more than twenty years, and almost 80 percent for more than ten years. A solid majority of the respondents had resided there for virtually the whole of their adult lives.[1] The preponderance of long-term residents is still evident at Paskwaw, although it is not as marked as at Osprey Lake. The other end of the residency spectrum also deserves notice, however. The MAA as well as the MDB and some settlers have accused the settlements of being less than welcoming to new applicants. The figures of 10 percent for Osprey Lake and 23 percent for

Paskwaw of members with less than five years of residency suggest that this charge may be less valid than is sometimes supposed.

Table 18
Duration of Residence

Osprey Lake			
Duration	Number	Percentage	Cumulative Percentage
Less than 5 years	5	10.0	10.0
5-10 years	4	8.0	18.0
11-20 years	8	16.0	34.0
More than 20 years	11	22.0	56.0
Whole life	20	40.0	96.0
No answer	2	4.0	100.0
Total	50	100.0	100.0
Paskwaw			
Less than 5 years	10	22.7	22.7
5-10 years	7	15.9	38.6
11-20 years	2	4.5	43.1
More than 20 years	12	27.3	70.4
Whole life	13	29.5	99.9
Total	44	99.9	99.9

The final demographic factor to be to be noted here is the level of unemployment on the two settlements. At the time of interview, 54 percent of the respondents at Osprey Lake and 63.6 percent of those at Paskwaw said they were without work. Since it was understood that questions about employment referred to paid employment, three points should be made. First, most women on the settlements neither hold nor aspire to hold jobs in the wage economy. Thus, the extent of unemployment suggested by these figures is undoubtedly exaggerated. Second, a number of the men, though not earning wage incomes, were in fact working to generate real income. The interviews at Osprey Lake were conducted at the height of the berry season, and plenty of men were working with the rest of the family to pick and preserve huge quantities of bush food. At Paskwaw, hunting trips on settlement land (which are legal at all seasons) were going on all the time. Finally, the fact that the interviews took place in the summer probably does not seriously distort the unemployment figures. Seasonal employment in the winter employs different people but not significantly fewer of them.

With this sketch of some of the demographic characteristics of the settlers, attention will now be given to their "external" political orientations, treating in order their orientations to the federal government, the provincial government, and the MAA. The FMSA is taken to be more "internal" than "external" to the government and politics of the settlements and is therefore discussed in the next chapter.

Orientations to the Federal Government

In response to the question, "Do you usually vote in federal elections?," thirty-one of fifty respondents (62 percent) at Osprey Lake and thirty-two of forty-four (73 percent) at Paskwaw answered "Yes." Moreover, twenty-eight (56 percent) of those at Osprey Lake and twenty-nine (66 percent) of those at Paskwaw said that they had voted in the most recent federal election (1980). The actual voter turnout in the Osprey Lake polling division was 48 percent and 42 percent at Paskwaw; the actual voter turnout for the whole of Alberta was 61 percent. The actual rates of turnout at the two settlements corresponded very closely to actual rates in other Native communities in north-central Alberta. Assuming that these samples are reasonably representative, a considerable number of the respondents on both settlements said that they had voted but had not in fact done so.[2] It is a common finding of students of voting that many people who say that they usually vote, or that they voted in a particular election, do not tell the truth. The standard explanation for this phenomenon is that they feel that as citizens they have a duty to vote. It is interesting to speculate whether the Metis share this sense of citizen duty.[3]

Table 19
Professed Voting of Respondents, 1980 Federal Election

Osprey Lake		
Political Party	Number	Percentage
Progressive Conservative	12	41.4
Liberal	10	34.4
NDP	5	17.2
Other	1	3.4
No answer	1	3.4
Total	29	99.8
Paskwaw		
Progressive Conservative	14	48.3
Liberal	2	6.9
NDP	7	24.1
No answer	6	20.7
Total	29	100.0

Table 19 shows the voting by party of the respondents on the two settlements who said they had voted in the 1980 election. This pattern of voting differs quite considerably from the pattern for Alberta as a whole, where in the 1980 election the Conservatives received 64 percent of the vote, the Liberals 22 percent, the NDP 10 percent, and others 4 percent. But it is much closer to the actual pattern in the Osprey Lake polling division, in which the Conservatives received 31 percent of the vote, the Liberals 42 percent, the NDP 18 percent, and others 10 percent. It is also somewhat closer to the pattern of voting in the federal riding in which Osprey Lake is situated. Nevertheless, the difference between the Osprey Lake pattern and that of the riding as a whole is quite striking. In the riding as a whole the Conservatives won an absolute majority of the votes, while the Liberals were not even close. Voting at Paskwaw also revealed deviance, but deviance of a different sort than that found at Osprey Lake.

The pattern of voting at Paskwaw (which is in the same large federal riding as Osprey Lake) also deviates significantly from the patterns in the province and in the riding. As at Osprey Lake, however, the actual pattern of voting in their own polling division resembles the recollections of the respondents. In fact, the Conservatives received 36 percent of the Paskwaw votes, the Liberals 31 percent, the NDP 26 percent, and others 7 percent. Both at Osprey Lake and at Paskwaw, respondents overstated their preference for the Conservative candidate and underestimated their preference for the Liberal. But at Osprey Lake the disparity, though significant, was not immense, whereas at Paskwaw it was huge. While 7 percent of the Paskwaw respondents said they had voted Liberal, 31 percent of the actual settlement vote was Liberal. Students of elections have found that, just as some voters say that they voted when in fact they did not, so some voters say that they voted for the winning candidate when they did not. This phenomenon is notable by its absence at Osprey Lake and Paskwaw. The Progressive Conservative candidate won the seat with ease, but the respondents in both settlements understated their preference for the winning candidate.

Respondents were asked a general question about their treatment by government, without reference to the difference between federal and provincial officials. Responses to this question will be discussed below in relation to orientations to the provincial government. However, they were questioned specifically about one federal agency, the RCMP. The question posed was the following: "Is the RCMP around here good, bad, or so-so?" At Osprey Lake the responses were "good," 60 percent, "so-so," 28 percent, and "bad," 10 percent; at Paskwaw they were "good," 43 percent, "so-so," 41 percent, and "bad," 14 percent. It is evident that the dominant view on both settlements is that the performance of the RCMP is satisfactory. It is clear, too, that the RCMP gets much higher grades from the residents of Osprey Lake than from those of Paskwaw. The explanation for their different evaluations coincide fully with those presented by the settlement councillors, which were discussed in Chapter 4. Except in a few instances, the quality of police personnel (including any propensity towards harassment based on ethnicity) was not seen as a factor. Negative judgements were based almost exclusively on insufficient rather than excessive or obtrusive policing. Paskwaw is less easily accessible than Osprey Lake from the nearest detachment, and Paskwaw residents were thus more inclined to complain about lack of regular patrolling and slow response to calls. At both settlements, but especially at Paskwaw, most residents would like to see more of the police, not less.

Orientations to the Provincial Government

In response to the question, "Do you usually vote in provincial elections?," forty-three of fifty respondents at Osprey Lake (86 percent) and twenty-four of forty-four at Paskwaw (55 percent) said that they did. Moreover, thirty-five (70 percent) of those at Osprey Lake and twenty-two (50 percent) of those at Paskwaw said that they had voted in the most recent provincial election (1982). The actual voter turnout both in the Osprey Lake and in the Paskwaw polling division was 42 percent. The apparent exaggeration at Osprey Lake on this matter is quite striking. The level of voter turnout in both settlements was well below the provincial average of 66 percent, but not so low compared to the average turnouts of the constituencies in which they are located. The level of turnout in the constituency in which Osprey Lake is located was only 51 percent and 57 percent in the constituency in which Paskwaw is located.

Table 20
Professed Voting of Respondents,
1982 Provincial Election

Osprey Lake		
Political Party	Number	Percentage
Progressive Conservative	18	51.4
Liberal	10	28.6
NDP	7	20.0
Total	35	100.0
Paskwaw		
Progressive Conservative	11	50.0
Liberal	1	4.5
NDP	8	36.4
Other	2	9.1
Total	22	100.0

Table 20 shows the voting by party of the respondents on the two settlements who said they had voted in the 1982 provincial election.

Respondents at Osprey Lake wildly overstated their support for the Liberal candidate and significantly understated their support for the candidates of the NDP and the separatist WCC. While 29 percent of the respondents said they had voted Liberal, only 2.7 percent of all the voters in Osprey Lake cast Liberal votes. Meanwhile, the NDP candidate received exactly the same number of votes as the Conservative (41 percent), while the WCC candidate got 15 percent. There is a plausible explanation for at least part of the exaggeration of the Liberal vote. The Liberal candidate was a Native, well known and highly esteemed on the settlement. It is possible that a number of settlers were unwilling to admit that they had not voted for him. The paucity of ethnic voting in Osprey Lake in the 1982 provincial election, combined with two other features of the vote there, give rise to an interesting speculation. In the constituency in which the settlement is located, 57 percent of the citizens voted Conservative, while only 41 percent of the settlement voters did so. The NDP also received 41 percent of the settlement vote, but only 29 percent of the vote of the constituency as a whole. This suggests that social class may be a salient factor in Osprey Lake voting behaviour—a hypothesis which is given further credence by the fact that the percentage of WCC voters at Osprey Lake was almost twice the constituency average: 15 percent as opposed to 8 percent.[4]

The correspondence between the recollections of the Paskwaw voters and the actual voting pattern of the settlement is almost perfect. The actual results in the poll were: Conservative, 46.8 percent; Liberal, 3.9 percent; NDP, 36.3 percent; other, 13.1 percent. It is noteworthy that in Paskwaw the respondents did not overstate their attachment to the Liberal candidate, who was not just a Native but a well-known Metis. Perhaps a partial explanation for this fact is that the Liberal candidate at Paskwaw was not held in such high regard as his counterpart in Osprey Lake. Certainly part of the explanation is that the Liberal was widely seen as a "parachute candidate," who had already lived in the city for several years by the time of the election. Perhaps more important, however, is the fact that the Paskwaw vote deviated from the provincial and the constituency norm in just the way that the Osprey Lake vote did. In the constituency in which Paskwaw is located, the Conservatives received 58 percent of the vote and the NDP only 17 percent, but on the settlement the Conservatives got only 47 percent compared to the NDP's 36 percent. This pattern was replicated on all but one of the Metis settlements and most of the Indian reserves in the northern part of the province. Once again, the possibility arises that voting based on considerations of social class is an important factor in Native communities.

All respondents on both settlements were asked three general questions (without distinction between the federal and provincial levels) about their perceptions of the performance of governments: "What about government people you deal with? Are they helpful, unhelpful, or so-so?"; "Which government people are most helpful?"; and "Which are least helpful?" Only 52 percent of the respondents at Osprey Lake and 21 percent of those at Paskwaw answered any of these questions. The size of the response at Osprey Lake is less impressive than it seems. In fact, only nine of the twenty-six interviewees who responded to one or more of the questions replied in such a way as to present a general evaluation of governmental performance combined with a discrimination of better and worse governmental agents and agencies. The rest either contented themselves with expressing their generally favourable attitude towards governments, without mentioning particular cases, or focussed on a single agency (usually the MDB) for praise or censure, without giving any kind of general assessment of governmental performance. Of the nine respondents at Paskwaw who answered one or more of the three questions about governmental performance, only four gave sophisticated responses that combined general with particular evaluations. That only 9 percent of the population of a community is fairly sophisticated in the evaluation of government is perhaps not unusual, but it is surprising that only one of every five of the Paskwaw respondents expressed *either* a general view about the performance of governments *or* some specific view(s) about the conduct of individual government agents or agencies. At the very least, one would have expected a number of comments (as at Osprey Lake) about the MDB or its officials. The responses at Paskwaw suggest that the community is not very attentive to the activities of off-settlement governments.

Although the difference is not reflected in participation rates in federal and provincial elections, the residents of Osprey Lake seem to be considerably more attentive to the activities of off-settlement governments than those of Paskwaw. Standard voting studies suggest that levels of attention to, and information about, government and politics are correlated with levels of schooling, and it has been seen that educational attainments at Osprey Lake are significantly higher than at Paskwaw. It has also been suggested that Paskwaw residents are more isolated geographically and more "traditional" culturally and economically than residents of Osprey Lake and other eastern settlements, and hence less interested in how the "outside world" impinges on them. The much higher level of Cree language retention and the possibly heavier reliance on hunting and trapping tend to support this claim. On the other hand, however, it appears that at least as high a proportion of

Paskwaw as of Osprey Lake residents work and engage in other activities off-settlement. The education argument seems to be highly plausible but the culture argument is at best unproved.

Orientations to the MAA

In the discussion of the political leaders of the settlements and the FMSA, it was seen that relationships with the MAA give rise to some controversy. In this section some figures will be presented (see Table 21) concerning respondents' past and present membership in the MAA, as well as their opinions concerning its performance.

Table 21
Membership in MAA

Osprey Lake		
Membership Status	Number	Percentage
Now a member	22	44.0
Previously a member	12	24.0
Never a member	16	32.0
Total	50	100.0
Paskwaw		
Now a member	22	50.0
Previously a member	12	27.3
Never a member	10	22.7
Total	44	100.0

The most significant factor here may be the minority that retains membership, rather than the majority that does not or the sizeable proportion that has allowed its membership to lapse.

At Paskwaw an even higher proportion of respondents are MAA members. However, these figures do not speak for themselves. There are a number of reasons, unrelated to politics, why a settlement member might choose to acquire or retain membership in the MAA, such as the opportunity to participate in congenial social gatherings. The crucial question regarding the political salience of the MAA on the settlements has to do with its perceived performance as a political organization. With this in mind, respondents were asked: "Do you think the MAA does a good job?" At both Osprey Lake and Paskwaw, 48 percent of the respondents felt unable to answer this question. On the other hand, 20 percent of the respondents at Osprey Lake and 25 percent at Paskwaw said that the MAA was doing a good job, while 16 percent of respondents at Osprey Lake and 7 percent at Paskwaw gave mixed reviews ("so-so," "good in some ways but poor in others," "helpful to Metis off-settlement but not much use to us," and so on). Finally, 16 percent of respondents at Osprey Lake and 21 percent at Paskwaw said that the MAA was not doing a good job. On the face of it, these figures suggest that most residents of these settlements were largely indifferent to the MAA. This impression might be reinforced by the observation that few of the negative comments about the MAA were expressed with strong feelings of hostility or resentment. Most of the respondents who found shortcomings in the MAA were not very worried about them. However, the picture is not so simple. Almost all of the respondents who thought the MAA was doing a good job stated their opinions with considerable intensity. Most of them held one or more of the following views: that some of the programs offered by the MAA were very valuable; that political alliance between the settlements and the MAA is mutually beneficial; and that the settlements owed it to other Metis, especially but not exclusively those residing in isolated communities, to collaborate with the MAA in working for their well-being.

All things considered, the residents of the Metis settlements interviewed in the course of this study seem to be slightly less informed and less concerned about political events and processes outside their own communities than would be a cross section of the general public. A comparatively low level of such information and concern would be expected if the settlers had a strong sense of their own distinctiveness and thereby an unusual preoccupation with the goings-on in their own communities. If that were the case, we should expect our respondents to be comparatively well informed and deeply concerned about the politics of their own settlements. The orientations of the Metis settlers to "internal" government and politics are considered in the next chapter.

NOTES

1. Occasional periods of employment off the settlement and longer periods away occasioned by service in the armed forces are taken to be consistent with this statement.
2. To the extent that our samples are unrepresentative, they should exaggerate rather than underestimate voting turnout. Our sample underrepresents younger voters, but numerous studies indicate that older voters are more likely to cast their ballots than younger ones.
3. To the author's knowledge, no Canadian survey has studied whether there are ethnic differences in the possession or strength of a belief in a citizen's duty to vote.
4. In the 1986 provincial election the NDP candidate (who won the seat) received 53 percent of the vote at Osprey Lake, compared to 26 percent for the Conservative. However, in the 1989 provincial election a Metis candidate running as a Conservative won the seat and was supported overwhelmingly by Osprey Lake voters, receiving 53 percent of the vote compared to 21 percent for the NDP incumbent.

8

Internal Political Orientations of the Metis Settlers

A major concern of this study is the feasibility and desirability of increased political self-determination for the Metis settlements. One requisite that must be met by a community that seeks a greater scope of self-government is that its members favour it. It is also necessary that the community be politically sound before serious thought is given to expanding its authority. The political health of a community has, of course, several dimensions. This chapter examines the attitudes, opinions and activities of "rank-and-file" community members. At present a politically healthy community does not lack political controversy and other forms of political conflict. On the contrary, a community free of political conflict is likely to be one in which dissent is suppressed. However, if the divisions within a community are deep and intense, it is unlikely to be able to maintain without continuous outside intervention a tolerably high level of political stability, much less an acceptable level of practical adherence to democratic norms. Thus, the political health of a community implies two things: the presence and open expression of political conflicts, and an underlying consensus strong and inclusive enough that conflicts are manageable in ways compatible with democratic norms. Although the discussion that follows is wide-ranging, these two concerns are meant to give it an underlying coherence. Particular attention is paid to three indicators of healthy conflict within consensus: that community members are well informed about matters pertaining to its political life; that they have considered opinions about community political issues; and that they participate in the political activities of the community.

General Orientations to Settlement Life

The discussion of the political activities, opinions and attitudes of the settlers begins by considering some of their feelings about settlement life. General sentiments about the quality of life in a community are not generally regarded as matters of "government" or "politics" in the narrow senses of these terms, but there can be no doubt that such sentiments are politically relevant in a broader sense. Levels of satisfaction within a community give some hints as to the performance of political institutions and leaders in responding to people's needs and aspirations. Accordingly, each of the respondents was asked: "Do you like living on this settlement?" The replies were overwhelmingly affirmative: 92 percent of the respondents at Osprey Lake gave an unequivocal "yes" and another 4 percent said "yes, with a few reservations." The corresponding figures at Paskwaw were 87 percent and 11 percent. Only two respondents at Osprey Lake and one at Paskwaw said that they did not like living on the settlement.

The respondents were then asked what they saw as the best things about settlement life. After reflection, 88 percent of the respondents at Osprey Lake and 98 percent of those at Paskwaw gave one or more reasons for enjoying settlement life, mentioning the tranquillity of the setting or the pace of life, a preference for rural over urban life, the low cost of living, and the legality of hunting in all seasons. However, many of the respondents concluded simply by saying "Well, it's *home*, you know," with a look that suggested that anyone who could understand that answer would not have asked the question in the first place. This, for most settlers, would appear to be *the* answer to the question of what is good about settlement life. This is not to suggest some romantic vision of the settlements as havens of community of man with man and nature. There are conflicts on the settlements, but a feeling for the nature and sources of those conflicts is part of the meaning of "it's home." The Metis have a distinctive culture, that culture permeates settlement life, and the settlers cherish it. This fact is crucial to an understanding of the politics of the settlements. The overriding concern of the vast majority of the settlers is that the conditions for maintaining and enhancing their distinctive way of life are ensured. For the most part, political consensus obtains to the extent that there is agreement on those conditions and the best way of ensuring them, and political conflict arises when there is disagreement either about the conditions or about the appropriate way to secure them.

Respondents were also asked, "Are there any things you don't like about the settlement?" This question met with strikingly different response rates on the two settlements: 78 percent of the respondents at Osprey Lake but only 32 percent of those at Paskwaw found fault with their respective communities. Respondents in both settlements expressed an extraordinarily wide range of complaints. In fact, a majority of the grievances on each settlement were mentioned by only one or two respondents. At Osprey Lake, only three complaints were expressed by 10 percent or more of the interviewees: the high level of unemployment (22 percent); the prevalence of favouritism, especially on the part of the settlement council (20 percent); and the number of able-bodied people relying on welfare. At Paskwaw, only one complaint was expressed by 10 percent of the respondents, who found the overall performance of the settlement council so unsatisfactory as to detract from the quality of life in the settlement.

The conclusion to be drawn from the responses to these general questions about the feelings of Osprey Lake and Paskwaw settlers concerning the quality of settlement life is that they appear to be quite contented. In particular, there seems to be no grievance on either settlement that has undermined the sense of well-being of the settlers. It remains to be seen whether this picture holds up as we examine the responses to some more pointed and more narrowly political questions.

Opinions About the Election and Performance of Settlement Councils

The respondents on each settlement were asked if they usually voted in settlement council elections. At Osprey Lake, 92 percent said that they did, as did 61 percent at Paskwaw. They were asked further if they had voted in the most recent settlement election, and the affirmative responses were 60 percent at Osprey Lake and 50 percent at Paskwaw. The rate of turnout in the most recent Paskwaw election was in fact just under 50 percent. A reliable comparison between the alleged and the actual turnout at Osprey Lake cannot be presented, since a by-election was held shortly after the regular election—respondents were not asked to distinguish between voting in the by-election and in the regular election. However, the percentage who said that they had voted in the "last" election was exactly the percentage that voted in the last *regular* election (60 percent). It should be noted that the rate of participation has been increasing steadily on both settlements.

The respondents were asked next what qualities they looked for in a candidate for election to the settlement council. Forty-five (90 percent) of the respondents at Osprey Lake and thirty-three (75 percent) of those at Paskwaw answered this question. The leading quality sought by respondents on both settlements was "fairness," which here means a disposition not to favour one's friends or family. At Osprey Lake the next most frequently mentioned virtue of a councillor was "independence," by which the respondents referred to a forthright commitment to principles strong enough to resist pressures not only from friends and family but also from other influential groups. Independence was also mentioned as an important quality for aspiring councillors by respondents at Paskwaw, but not nearly so frequently as at Osprey Lake. The quality placed second at Paskwaw was "honesty," which was also mentioned by a number of respondents at Osprey Lake. There were two principal differences between the settlements regarding professed grounds for assessing candidates. First, a much higher proportion of the respondents at Osprey Lake attached importance to formal educational attainments. Second, at Osprey Lake there was a widely shared view that a council should contain a blend of youth and experience, a matter of concern for very few Paskwaw respondents.

When asked what qualities they felt others on the settlement looked for when voting for a member of council, 22 percent of respondents at Osprey Lake and 43 percent at Paskwaw said that they did not know. A further 22 percent at Osprey Lake, and 16 percent at Paskwaw, believed that others looked for the same qualities as they did themselves, while only 4 percent of the respondents at Osprey Lake and 7 percent at Paskwaw attributed to other voters motives different from their own. However, 52 percent of the Osprey Lake respondents and 34 percent of those at Paskwaw felt that most participants in settlement elections voted for their friends or, even more commonly, members of their families. There are a number of differences between the two settlements in the pattern of their responses to the question under consideration, but there is also a striking similarity. On both settlements more than twice as many respondents felt that others based their voting on grounds of friendship or family connections, rather than on the public-spirited criteria they employed themselves. This kind of response is by no means peculiar to Metis settlements, but what is surprising is the extraordinary political salience attributed by the settlers to family ties. We have seen evidence of the settlers' worries about the political role of family ties in relation to concerns about favouritism on the part of candidates for settlement council, and again in relation to concerns about the motivation of voters. We will return to this matter later in the present chapter, since it is crucial to understanding the political outlooks of the settlers.

Turning from the selection of settlement councils to their performance, respondents were asked if they thought their council was doing a good job. Replies to this question are presented in Table 22. In reply to this general question, the Osprey Lake respondents gave their council fairly high grades. However, the fact that one in three said that the council was not doing a good job is not to be dismissed lightly, especially in view of the ample opportunity they were given to assess the council's performance as "so-so." As Table 22 indicates, the pattern of responses at Paskwaw was not strikingly different.

Table 22
Performance of Settlement Council

Osprey Lake

Quality of Performance	Number	Percentage
Good	23	46.0
So-so	10	20.0
Not good	16	32.0
Don't know/no answer	1	2.0
Total	50	100.0

Paskwaw

	Number	Percentage
Good	22	50.0
So-so	10	22.7
Not good	8	18.2
Don't know/no answer	4	9.1
Total	44	100.0

With a view to eliciting more specific evaluations of the councils, respondents were then asked two questions: "Is there anything particularly good about the council or things it does especially well?" and "Is there anything particularly bad about the council, or things it does especially badly?" At Osprey Lake, all but three of the respondents answered one or both of these questions. Twenty-eight of the respondents said that the council did have specific strengths, but a number of them gave no concrete examples, affirming that it was very effective in all aspects of its work. Among those who identified specific merits of the council, almost as many strengths were mentioned as people who mentioned them. It was commended for qualities as diverse as fairness, willingness to stand up to the MDB, industriousness, and the provision of excellent recreational programs. Three merits were mentioned somewhat more frequently than others: vigorous and effective handling of matters of economic development; responsiveness to settlers' requests; and success in improving the quantity, quality and criteria for distribution of housing. Thirty-five of the respondents said that their council had specific weaknesses. Comments about council shortcomings were much more focussed than those about strengths, with a high proportion of respondents making one or more of three specific complaints. First, 40 percent of those who found fault with the council said that some or all of its members engaged in favouritism, with their own families or members of the "leading families" on the settlement being the principal recipients of favoured treatment. Second, 31 percent of the complainants felt that the council was not sufficiently open to suggestions from settlers or vigorous enough in seeking out suggestions from them. Finally, 26 percent felt that the council was guilty of sins both of commission and omission in regard to economic development.

In striking contrast, twenty of the forty-four respondents at Paskwaw (45 percent) could identify neither a specific merit nor a specific defect of their settlement council. Only eleven (25 percent) attempted to describe the good qualities of their council, and the most common compliment (mentioned by four of eleven) was that "they try hard." Twenty Paskwaw respondents (45 percent) found shortcomings in their council. As at Osprey Lake, favouritism led the list of council defects, mentioned by seven (35 percent) of the Paskwaw respondents who had specific complaints. Also mentioned by 35 percent of respondents was another complaint heard frequently at Osprey Lake, the lack of consultation of community members by councillors. The only other noteworthy complaint, mentioned by four respondents, had to do with the poor organization and excessive length of meetings.

Table 23
Responsiveness of Settlement Council

Osprey Lake		
Level of Responsiveness*	Number	Percentage
High	29	58.0
Medium	6	12.0
Low	14	28.0
Don't know/no answer	1	2.0
Total	50	100.0
Paskwaw		
High	21	47.7
Medium	10	22.7
Low	11	25.0
Don't know/no answer	2	4.5
Total	44	99.9

*The categories "High," "Medium," and "Low" are based on answers to the question, "Do you feel that members of the council listen to you if you have advice or complaints?" High = unequivocal or emphatic "yes"; Medium = "sometimes" or "it depends" (e.g., on the councillor or the type of issue); Low = unequivocal or emphatic "no."

Both at Paskwaw and at Osprey Lake, favouritism and lack of communication and responsiveness were the most frequently mentioned criticisms of the settlement councils. Fortunately, the questionnaire that guided the interviews contained additional questions pertaining to these very matters. Favouritism will be taken up later in the chapter. Here the matter of responsiveness is addressed in the respondents' answers to the question: "Do you feel that members of the council listen to you if you have advice or complaints?" As is seen in Table 23, posing a specific question about responsiveness elicits a much higher response rate, and therefore provides a more reliable judgement on the extent to which lack of responsiveness is seen as a serious problem.

An interesting anomaly presents itself here. In reply to an open-ended question about shortcomings of their council, lack of responsiveness was mentioned by eleven of the respondents at Osprey Lake. But in reply to a specific question about responsiveness, only fourteen ranked it as low. The hypothesis suggests that there might be an easily identifiable group of people who would perceive the council as unresponsive, that is, members of small families who might have seen the council as dominated by the leading families. This hypothesis is not supported by the evidence of these interviews. Members of the three "leading families" at Osprey Lake formed a disproportionately large segment of those who found the council low in responsiveness. Indeed, a senior member of the settlement's largest family (who is widely regarded as the most influential person on the settlement) was among those who maintained that the council's principal shortcoming was that its ablest members spent too much time and energy dealing with the provincial government, and too little consulting with ordinary settlers.

The pattern of responses at Paskwaw was very similar to that at Osprey Lake. Seven respondents complained about unresponsiveness in reply to an open-ended question, but in answer to a specific question about responsiveness, only eleven gave their council a low rating. Once again, members of the leading families were as likely to complain about unresponsiveness as were others.[1] It would appear on the basis of the interviews that a solid majority on each settlement regards its council as reasonably responsive, but that a sizeable minority feels strongly that its council is seriously defective in regard to its attentiveness to ordinary settlers.

Opinions Regarding Problems Facing the Settlements

One of the most important dimensions of the settlers' orientations towards settlement government and politics is their identification of problems facing the settlement, particularly the relative importance they attribute to the problems they see. Accordingly, respondents were asked: "What is the biggest problem facing the settlement nowadays?"

On both settlements there was overwhelming consensus that unemployment was the biggest problem they faced. At Osprey Lake, 42 percent of the respondents saw this as the biggest problem. Only two other problems, lack of funds for economic development and council favouritism, were identified by as many as 8 percent. At Paskwaw, 41 percent saw unemployment as the biggest problem, and the only other reply given by more than one interviewee was the "don't know" given by six (14 percent) of the respondents. When asked about the second biggest problem facing the settlements, the "don't know" category rose from 4 percent to 26 percent at Osprey Lake, and from 14 percent to 39 percent at Paskwaw. But once again unemployment easily topped the list at both settlements, seen as the second biggest problem by 20 percent of the respondents at Osprey Lake and 16 percent at Paskwaw. Thus, 62 percent of the respondents at Osprey Lake and 57 percent at Paskwaw saw unemployment as either the biggest or the second biggest problem on their settlements. Once again, no more than one Paskwaw respondent mentioned any other problem. Six Osprey Lake respondents saw problems concerning education, and five saw shortcomings in the quantity and quality of housing, as their second biggest problem. Finally, respondents were asked if there were any other major problems facing their settlements. No other problems were mentioned by more than one Paskwaw respondent, but five more from Osprey Lake mentioned unemployment. These figures speak for themselves. According to the respondents at both settlements, unemployment dwarfs in importance all other problems.

Opinions About Self-Government

The issue of self-government has become a prominent one in Native politics, among the Metis as well as the Indians and the Inuit. But the attention given to this issue by scholars and by journalists has focussed almost exclusively on the views of Native leaders, especially spokespersons for prominent provincial, regional, territorial and national organizations. We know very little about the views of Native people who do not occupy prominent positions. Respondents were asked: "Would the settlement be better off if it were freer to make its own decisions without government interference?" Note that this question does not contain the term "self-government." The point of the actual phrasing was to avoid forcing respondents to make a stark choice either for or against something that does not have a definite meaning. (How wide a scope of jurisdiction, and how much autonomy within that jurisdiction, must a community have in order to be described as self-governing?) In the interviews the choice was left open for respondents to opt for greater or lesser "degrees" of freedom from government intervention in matters relating to the settlements. In what follows the term "self-government" will be used from time to time for the sake of brevity, but the qualifications noted above should be kept in mind. Responses to the question about increased political autonomy for the settlements are presented in Table 24.

Table 24
Opinions About Self-Government

Osprey Lake

Strength of Support or Opposition	Number	Percentage	Cumulative Percentage
Unqualified yes	8	16	16.0
Qualified yes	7	14	30.0
Qualified no	12	24	54.0
Unqualified no	18	36	90.0
Don't know/no answer	5	10	100.0
Total	50	100	100.0

Paskwaw

	Number	Percentage	Cumulative Percentage
Unqualified yes	13	29.5	29.5
Qualified yes	5	11.4	40.9
Qualified no	3	6.8	47.7
Unqualified no	14	31.8	79.5
Don't know/no answer	9	20.5	100.0
Total	44	100.0	100.0

Perhaps the most striking difference between the pattern of responses at Paskwaw and that at Osprey Lake is the much higher proportion of interviewees at Paskwaw who gave no answer to the question. Otherwise, the shapes of the distributions are not remarkably dissimilar. However, the question does arise whether it is more appropriate to emphasize the relatively high proportion of respondents who opposed increased political autonomy or the relatively low proportion who opposed it without qualification.

The figures in these tables do not speak for themselves and a brief commentary on the meaning of the various answers is required. The first thing that needs to be understood is that even settlement and FMSA leaders do not engage in rhetoric about "sovereignty." Nor do they take seriously talk about quasi-provincial status. On the other hand, proponents of an increased level of political autonomy for the settlements do have in mind a broader scope of jurisdiction than is enjoyed by municipalities. They believe that the settlements can and should take over all, or almost all, of the functions of the MDB. Typically, their belief is that the MDB as such should be abolished and most of its functions transferred to the settlements and the FMSA and agencies created by them, with the Metis agencies having more direct access to top decision makers within the provincial government, particularly to the deputy minister and the minister of Municipal Affairs. Thus, those who answered the "self-government" question with an unqualified "yes" were essentially stating their belief that the settlements were already capable of assuming this increased authority.

The difference between those who answered with a "qualified yes" and those who answered with a "qualified no" was one of degree, but the difference of degree was so large that it would be misleading to lump them into a single category. A "qualified yes" indicated that the respondent believed that the settlements could and should assume expanded authority in the near future. The most common reason for favouring a delay was the belief that the settlements and the FMSA needed more time to train and organize a capable group of managers before they could handle effectively a wider range of responsibilities. In contrast, those who answered with a "qualified no" believed that an extended delay would be required before the settlements were capable of exercising broader responsibilities. Many of them, too, saw the development of a cadre of capable managers as a prerequisite to increased political autonomy, but they believed that the achievement of this goal would take several years. Some of them also saw many of their political leaders as unfit for greater responsibilities, most commonly because of a lack of formal education or a propensity to engage in favouritism to the advantage of family and friends. They did not see these shortcomings as remediable in the short run, but believed that they would be overcome in time. For those responding with a "qualified no," increased autonomy was decidedly a long-term objective.

Those who answered the "self-government" question with an "unqualified no" were simply distrustful of their present and prospective political leaders. A minority of this group held that Native people are simply incapable of governing themselves effectively and fairly. But the largest proportion of this group maintained that the strength of family bonds was so powerful among Metis people that increased self-government, with no appeal to disinterested outsiders, would intensify and legitimize nepotism.

Consideration must now be given to the question of whether it is more appropriate to emphasize the relatively large proportion of respondents who were opposed to increased political self-determination, or the relatively small proportion who were *strongly* opposed to it. It would appear that neither of these points should be emphasized to the exclusion of the other. It is politically significant that a solid majority of the respondents on each settlement who had an opinion on the subject were either supportive of increased political autonomy or at least not adamantly opposed to its eventual implementation. But it is also important that a very sizeable minority on each settlement was strongly opposed to any enhancement of political autonomy and that a smaller but by no means insignificant group saw the implementation of greater political autonomy as desirable eventually but not in the near future. Leaving aside temporarily considerations of political ethics, political prudence evidently counsels against hasty movement towards self-government.[2] If the seemingly reasonable view is taken that major and rapid steps in the direction of increased self-government should be supported by a strong consensus, it must be said that both the proponents and the opponents are faced with a major political selling job.

Orientations to the FMSA

Before returning to the issue of favouritism, a few words should be said about the settlers' orientations to the FMSA, since it is regarded by most councillors as a major contributor to the well-being of the settlements. Respondents were asked four questions about the FMSA: "Are you familiar with the FMSA?"; "Do you think the FMSA does a good job?"; "Can you think of any ways it could do a better job?"; and "Do you think the president of the FMSA has done a good job?"

The most striking feature of the replies to these questions is the remarkable difference between the Osprey Lake and Paskwaw respondents in their respective rates of response. At Paskwaw 52 percent of the respondents, compared to 22 percent at Osprey Lake, were not familiar with the FMSA *at all.* (It should be kept in mind that these figures exclude those who had heard of the FMSA but knew little or nothing about it.) At the other extreme, 50 percent of the respondents at Osprey Lake, but only 34 percent at Paskwaw, claimed to be familiar with the FMSA. At Osprey Lake 58 percent of the respondents, compared to 34 percent at Paskwaw, were able to comment on the performance of the FMSA, while 40 percent at Osprey Lake, in contrast to 9 percent at Paskwaw, made suggestions as to how the FMSA could do a better job. Finally, 52 percent of the respondents at Osprey Lake, but only 23 percent of those at Paskwaw, were prepared to comment on the performance of the then president of the FMSA. (Readers who choose to reflect on these figures might wish to note that the then president of the FMSA was from a western settlement and that his immediate successor was to be a resident of Paskwaw.) The higher response rate at Osprey Lake than at Paskwaw was not confined to questions about the FMSA. The response rate at Paskwaw was lower, and often markedly lower, on every question concerning settlers' orientations to settlement government and politics, but nowhere else was the contrast so dramatic as in regard to questions about the FMSA. The lower response rate may lend some support to the contention of a number of informed observers that residents of the western settlements are less knowledgeable and less engaged politically than those in the east.

It may seem odd, on first consideration, that the few respondents at Paskwaw tended to be much more favourably disposed towards the FMSA than their more numerous counterparts at Osprey Lake. At Paskwaw, 73 percent of the respondents who answered the question thought that the FMSA was doing a good job, as opposed to 62 percent at Osprey Lake. Only 27 percent of the Paskwaw respondents who expressed an opinion could think of ways in which the FMSA could do a better job, compared to 69 percent at Osprey Lake. Finally, 80 percent at Paskwaw, but only 42 percent at Osprey Lake, stated unequivocally that the president of the FMSA was doing a good job. However, closer examination of the interview data alleviates the surprise one may feel on finding that the Paskwaw respondents were considerably more supportive of the FMSA. There are two main elements in the explanation. First, the Paskwaw respondents were highly politicized and, more often than not, former members of the settlement council. Accordingly, they were better informed about the FMSA and therefore more aware of the advantages it brought to the settlements. Second, the seemingly lower approval given to the FMSA by the Osprey Lake respondents is in a way misleading. The fact that many respondents at Osprey Lake suggested ways in which the FMSA could do a better job was not, in most cases, an expression of hostility towards it but rather an expression of genuine concern that it should improve. Similarly, negative assessments of the FMSA president by Osprey Lake respondents appear less so when examined more closely. For one thing, a much higher proportion of Osprey Lake than Paskwaw respondents who evaluated the president's performance (seven of twenty-six, or 27 percent, versus one of ten, or 10 percent) saw his work as good in some respects and not good in others. As well, several of the Osprey Lake respondents who did not think that the president did a good job acknowledged that there were aspects of his performance that were commendable. It was not uncommon to hear comments like: "He made too many decisions on his own, but he was a good speaker," "He was too concerned with his own political ambitions, but he was never afraid to stand up to the MDB," and "He didn't spend enough time on the settlements, but he knew how to deal with politicians and bureaucrats." It can be concluded that, in regard to the FMSA as in several other matters, the respondents at Osprey Lake tended to be politically more attentive and more sophisticated than those at Paskwaw. Having said that, however, it should be added that the low level of familiarity with the FMSA on both settlements should be a matter of concern to settlement and FMSA leaders.[3]

The Issue of Favouritism

The issue of favouritism (and the related issue of nepotism) has arisen several times already but deserves more intensive treatment. Of course favouritism is by no means confined to Metis or Native communities. Apart from political patronage, with which most people are all too familiar, favouritism is frequently present in the "private" sector, with the rewarding of friends and kin (such as the son-in-law who "works his way up from the top"). It may well be that favouritism, although it is more visible in Native communities because it operates through manifestly political decisions, is at least as widespread in the dominant society when private-sector as well as public-sector partiality is taken into account.

Table 25
Perceived Favouritism

Osprey Lake			
Belief that Favouritism is Practised	Number	Percentage	Cumulative Percentage
Unqualified yes	29	58	58.0
Qualified yes	6	12	70.0
Qualified no	5	10	80.0
Unqualified no	7	14	94.0
Don't know/no answer	3	6	100
Total	50	100	100.0
Paskwaw			
Unqualified yes	22	50.0	50.0
Qualified yes	7	15.9	65.9
Qualified no	5	11.4	77.3
Unqualified no	7	15.9	93.2
Don't know/no answer	3	6.8	100.0
Total	44	100.0	100.0

The final question posed to the settler respondents was: "I have heard it said that if you're looking for something like a job on the settlement or a new house, it helps to be related to a council member. Do you agree?" Responses to this question are presented in Table 25.

Obviously, favouritism is widely perceived to be a fact of life at both Osprey Lake and Paskwaw. The similarities between Osprey Lake and Paskwaw regarding perceived favouritism are such that the small differences are not worthy of comment. At Paskwaw, as at Osprey Lake, a solid majority saw favouritism as endemic. In these tables the labels "unqualified yes" and "unqualified no" require no interpretation. The difference between "qualified yes" and "qualified no" is one of degree, but the degree is large. It would be highly misleading to collapse these two categories into one. The emphasis of those who attached a qualification to their "no" answer was that, while favouritism was still very much a part of settlement life, some efforts were being made—if only by some councillors—to reduce if not eliminate it. The implication, however, was that their efforts were usually unsuccessful. In contrast, the emphasis of those who attached a qualification to their "yes" answer was that, while favouritism and nepotism had once been a prominent feature of life on their settlement, it now occurred only in isolated instances. That is, they did not deny that there were cases of favouritism, but they maintained that for the most part their council distributed advantages impartially according to reasonable and public criteria. In the interest of representing the views of the respondents accurately, it should be noted that a number of respondents from all categories agreed with part of the assessment of those who answered with a "qualified no," that favouritism was neither as widespread nor as severe as it had been in earlier days.

Two kinds of nepotism (favouritism) need to be distinguished—micro-nepotism and macro-nepotism. Micro-nepotism refers to the practice wherein a council member (or two or more related councillors) ensure—with at least the tacit assent of the other members of council—that a friend or a family member receives a benefit (a house, a well, a job, financial assistance for educational upgrading) in preference to a better-qualified, more deserving, or needier applicant. Micro-nepotism thus operates more or less sporadically, in that it comes into play only when a friend or family member of a council member seeks preferential treatment. Macro-nepotism is the practice wherein members of the "leading families" are persistent, "institutionalized" recipients of favoured treatment.

The matter of macro-nepotism requires some elaboration. According to informed observers—including members of the stigmatized/envied families themselves, as well as other residents and knowledgeable outsiders—a few families on each settlement are especially influential.[4] Their special influence stems from a variety of factors, such as size, historical roots in the settlement, and distinguished accomplishments of family members. They exercise their influence, often in collusion with each other, in such ways as deciding which potential issues become real issues within the community, excluding other potential issues from community discussion, recruiting and supporting candidates for settlement office, and rewarding their allies. The leading families receive favoured treatment as individuals and sometimes as collectivities, regardless of the composition of the settlement council. That is, they receive a disproportionate share of the benefits from the council, whether or not their own kin numerically dominate it.

Fuller understanding of macro-nepotism may be aided by a more concrete description, drawn from Osprey Lake, where complaints about macro-nepotism are more frequent than at Paskwaw. Observers maintain that there are four leading families at Osprey Lake: the Greggs, who constitute 20 percent of the settlement's entire population; the Allens (6 percent); the Brights (12 percent); and the Cliches (6 percent). The members of all these families are held to be beneficiaries of micro-nepotism (the Brights, who are regarded as latecomers, less so than the others), because they so frequently have kinfolk on the council. However, they are also said to benefit from macro-nepotism in two ways. First, council members are said to treat members of these families with special attention and generosity even when they are not kinfolk. For example, the Greggs are said to receive more than their fair share of new houses, regardless of how many Greggs sit on council. Second, the leading families are said to act in collusion to induce council to maintain practices conducive to them. For example, a very sizeable proportion of the good land at Osprey Lake is reserved as pasture land for the Stockbreeders' Association. The dominant members of the Stockbreeders' Association are Greggs and Allens. Successive settlement councils have firmly resisted efforts by settlers who are not members of the leading families to shrink the allotment of pasture land to the Stockbreeders' Association and put it to uses deemed by the others as more beneficial to the community as a whole. The Cliches are rewarded with the trappings of elected office and with the maintenance of educational upgrading programs—benefits more to their taste than preferential treatment in the sphere of agriculture. The Brights, the least influential and prestigious of the leading families, must content themselves with positive discrimination in the realm of council-controlled employment opportunities.

At Paskwaw, complaints tended to centre more on micro-nepotism. In particular, respondents spoke of instances in which individuals were elected to council on a platform of bringing new ideas and new blood to settlement affairs, only to resign in midterm after getting new houses for themselves or members of their families. However, macro-nepotism was also observed at Paskwaw. Three families leading families were seen there: the Millers (who constituted 13 percent of the settlement's population), the Chretiens (7 percent), and the Lapointes (14 percent). No institution like the Stockbreeders' Association at Osprey Lake was seen as their special preserve but, as at Osprey Lake, the leading families at Paskwaw were seen as recipients of a disproportionate share of the benefits in the gift of the settlement council, regardless of its composition.

Since charges of favouritism were so pervasive on both settlements, it was necessary to try to find out if they were well founded. The first method used was the crude one of "eyeball empiricism," which involved travelling around the two settlements to see if the members of the leading families typically lived in newer and better houses than other residents, and if they were more likely to have their own wells. It appeared, from these observations, that members of the leading families at Osprey Lake did not seem to enjoy better amenities than other residents. One example was particularly impressive. A number of respondents at Osprey Lake had complained that August Gregg, a man in his mid-fifties who was said to be the leading member of the largest family, "ran the settlement." Although he had a well, his house was not new and showed no signs of recent major repair. However, he was a leading figure in the Stockbreeders' Association. He was asked whether he was, in this capacity, a beneficiary of special treatment by the settlement council, and the same question was put to members of the settlement council. Both Gregg and the council members acknowledged that Gregg benefited from the policy of protecting the pasture land of the Stockbreeders' Association, but both denied that the matter involved any kind of favouritism. Both affirmed that it was a matter of policy, sustained by a number of successive councils and defended in open forum, that the Stockbreeders' Association should be supported because it effectively pursued the economic activity (ranching) for which the settlement's land was best suited.

The considerations mentioned above are obviously not conclusive. However, as a more systematic test of the presence of favouritism, the chairman of the Osprey Lake council was asked for information on the allocation of new housing and wells, which the council secretary promptly provided for the preceding five-year period. This data revealed that members of the leading families received less than their proportionate share of both housing and wells during this period. It might be thought that this was an unreliable test since members of the leading families would have had these already. Two considerations militate against this hypothesis. First, members of the leading families complained as often as others about their lack of houses and wells. Second, and more important, proportionately as many members of the leading families as of other families were coming into adulthood, marrying and raising families, and eager to set up households separate from their parents, and thus requiring houses and wells. Once again, the evidence is not conclusive. There may be instances of favouritism at Osprey Lake, but the evidence suggests that there is no pattern of macro-nepotism.

The same tests were used at Paskwaw. Observation yielded the impression that members of the leading families at Paskwaw tended to be better housed than members of other families, but such impressions, as we have already noted, are unreliable.[5] Accordingly, the chairman of the settlement council was asked for specific information about the allocation of new houses and wells in the recent past. Although he had been friendly and helpful in other ways, he did not provide this information. The manager and the secretary of the settlement were then asked for the information but they were equally evasive, and the matter was not pursued further. Refusal to divulge information is not conclusive evidence of malfeasance, but it is interesting that the Osprey Lake council had declared publicly that its books were open to all residents of the settlement and had extended this openness to an outsider, while the Paskwaw council had not. There would appear to be reason to *suspect* that there is a good deal of favouritism at Paskwaw and rather little at Osprey Lake. At the very least, the policy of openness at Osprey Lake is better designed to combat charges of favouritism than is the guardedness at Paskwaw. In view of the widespread concerns about alleged favouritism on both settlements, the Osprey Lake policy is manifestly better designed to defuse a divisive political issue.

If, as was maintained at the beginning of this chapter, a major dimension of the political health of a community is that it exhibits conflict within consensus, both Osprey Lake and Paskwaw seem to be in good condition. As has been shown, there are a number of areas of disagreement and controversy on both settlements. The allocation of scarce goods by the settlement councils generates deep conflicts, especially when it is seen by many settlers to be influenced by nepotism or other types of favouritism, but even the most severe conflicts are moderated by an underlying consensus. Settlers sometimes disagree strongly with each other and with some or all members of their councils, but these disagreements do not create irreconcilable antagonisms. There is an underlying conviction that preservation of the settlements and the distinctive way of life they make possible is far more important than differences of opinion about specific policies, processes and institutions. Settlers are not above disparaging some of the motives of their neighbours and their politicians, but none expressed the slightest doubt about any other settler's devotion to the integrity of the settlement.

An examination of the three more specific indicators of political health identified at the beginning of the chapter—that the settlers be well informed about matters pertaining to the political life of their community, that they have lively opinions about community political issues, and that they participate in community political activities—reveals a spottier but still generally positive picture. Even the least-engaged politically of the respondents were reasonably well informed about political institutions and activities on the settlement. In particular, virtually no ignorance or confusion about the scope or limits of the settlement councils' authority were found. On the other hand, respondents on both settlements displayed a remarkable ignorance of the purposes and activities of the FMSA. Not surprisingly, lack of knowledge was accompanied by lack of opinion. Especially at Paskwaw, but also to a large extent at Osprey Lake, respondents had little idea of what the FMSA was doing on their behalf, and very few had specific opinions as to what the FMSA could do to improve its performance. If the settlements are to acquire a significantly enhanced level of political self-determination, it will certainly be necessary for them to rely heavily on a trans-settlement political body, be it the FMSA or a successor agency. If this body is to be responsive to the concerns of "ordinary" settlers, the latter will have to expand their sphere of attention beyond their own communities.

Excluding the FMSA, respondents tended to have vigorous opinions about settlement political issues. Even when they expressed "mixed" or "qualified" views about issues, they did so with some feeling. For example, a number of the respondents at Osprey Lake who judged the performance of their settlement council as "so-so" were outspoken both in their praise of some features of the council and in their condemnation of others. Similarly, a number of respondents at Paskwaw who gave "qualified" answers to the question about favouritism forcefully stated their reasons for doing so.

The level of participation at both settlements in community political activities is fairly high in comparison to participation rates in their most obvious analogues—urban and rural municipalities. Evidence to support comparisons is difficult to obtain, since the Alberta Department of Municipal Affairs does not keep records of electoral turnout. However, the fact that the turnout in the Edmonton civic election was 42 percent in 1983 and 20 percent in 1980, and in Red Deer 28 percent in 1983 and 39 percent in 1980 is suggestive.[6] A turnout rate of about 50 percent is respectable. Moreover, participation in general meetings is also quite high, comparing favourably with rates of attendance at meetings in city neighbourhoods facing critical situations. It is reasonable to conclude that the level of political activity found on the settlements, though not striking, is still reasonably high. On balance, the political health of the settlements, to the extent that it depends on the attitudes, opinions, and activities of "ordinary" residents, seems to be reasonably sound.

NOTES

1. The fact that members of the leading families on both settlements complained about unresponsiveness does not refute the claim that they occupy a privileged position. To mention just one possibility, it could be the case that they *expect* to be consulted more frequently and fully than others and therefore complain more readily.
2. This judgement is supported by further analysis of the survey data, which indicates that hostility to, and hesitancy about, increased political self-determination was not associated with age. There is no question of waiting for death to remove the opponents of self-government.
3. At both settlements the most common complaint about the FMSA was that settlers were given too little information about it.
4. The "reputational approach" to the study of community power relationships is not well received in political science and sociology. See, for example, Robert A. Dahl, "A Critique of the Ruling Elite Model," *American Political Science Review* (June 1958): 463-69. However, this discussion avoids the central criticism of that approach, that it is illegitimate to infer from the fact that "X" is *reputed* to be powerful that "X" really *is* powerful. We do not take the designation of a family as a "leading" family" as evidence that it is influential or advantaged.
5. Relying on impressions about housing is especially dangerous on the Metis settlements. New houses on the settlements are quite rudimentary, but owners can upgrade them by additional payment. Accordingly, it is easy to be more "impressed" by an older house that is comparatively elegant than by a new one that is Spartan.
6. Jack Masson, *Alberta's Local Governments and Their Politics* (Edmonton: University of Alberta Press, 1985), 331. It is difficult to comment on levels of electoral participation in towns, villages and rural municipalities because of the frequency of election by acclamation. With two exceptions, the candidates for mayor in all the towns near the Metis settlements were

acclaimed in 1983. Mayoralty elections were held in Bonnyville and Lac la Biche but not in Athabasca, Barrhead, Cold Lake, Elk Point, Grande Centre, High Level, High Prairie, Manning, Slave Lake, Swan Hills or St. Paul. In High Prairie, the town with the largest number of Metis settlements in near proximity, not only the mayor but all members of the town council were acclaimed.

9
The Self-Government Issue

Leaders of Canadian Native groups are increasingly seeking a greater scope of political self-determination. Leaders of the Alberta Metis settlements, especially as represented by the FMSA, are no exception. Should a right of self-government for the settlements be embodied in law (perhaps by way of constitutional entrenchment) and political practice with all deliberate speed? That is the question addressed in this chapter.

The most dramatic recent demands of Native organizations in the political realm are usually described as a quest for self-government. In this context, the term "political self-determination" would be more appropriate than the term "self-government." "Self-government" suggests a sharp "either/or" proposition. That is, it suggests that Native collectivities must be either fully self-governing or essentially colonized "wards of the state." This dichotomy is both logically and politically untenable. There are many gradations between complete self-government, as exhibited in sovereign statehood, and complete subjection to a superior authority, as exhibited in extreme forms of colonialism. In contrast, the term "political self-determination" suggests the possibility of gradations of degree or scope. That is, it suggests that the extent of the political autonomy of a community may be expanded or contracted in degree, so that it is possible to speak of increases or decreases in political self-determination. The term "self-government" will be used frequently in what follows, partly for the sake of brevity, partly to avoid monotonous repetition of a single phrase, and partly because its usage referring to the matters discussed is so widespread. It should be kept in mind, however, that "self-government," as used here, admits of degrees.

This matter of degrees of political self-determination is very much to the point in regard to discussions and negotiations relating to the self-government of the Alberta Metis settlements. On the one hand, settlement and FMSA spokespersons, unlike leaders of some other Native collectivities,[1] have avoided talk about sovereignty and similar rhetoric suggesting that they seek to dissociate themselves from the jurisdictions of the federal and provincial governments; rather, they have consistently maintained that they are, and wish to remain, public-spirited citizens of Canada and Alberta.[2] On the other hand, the Alberta government has refrained from portraying Metis politicians as separatists or quasi-separatists. Like the Metis politicians, provincial government officials have been willing to discuss increased political self-determination for the settlements on its merits, refraining from adopting extreme ideological stances or misrepresenting Metis aspirations. More specifically, they have been willing to discuss self-government for the settlements in light of its probable contribution to the well-being of the settlers, as well as other Albertans.

Three Approaches to the Issue of Native Self-Government

There are two dominant approaches to the issue of Native self-government: the legal approach and the rights-based approach. In this section these two approaches will be examined. It will then be argued that a third approach, the well-being approach, can remedy the shortcomings of the other two.

The Legal Approach

Those who employ the legal approach attempt to develop or undermine arguments for Native self-government by appealing to and interpreting practices, documents and rules that can be argued to have legal standing. Lawyers have already produced some innovative and interesting pieces on Native self-government.[3] Nevertheless, the legal approach need not detain us for long, due to its inherent philosophical and political limitations. The most that lawyers can do is tell us what can and cannot be done legally in regard to Native self-government. They cannot tell us whether Native people have a moral right to govern themselves. Nor can they tell us, in their professional capacity, whether or not it is desirable that Native people should enjoy greater political autonomy. Thus the legal approach is not able to deal with the central philosophical questions concerning Native self-government. Moreover, this approach has serious political as well as philosophical limitations. It is unlikely that a Canadian court will find that any group of aboriginal people has a surviving right to govern itself.[4] But even in the most unlikely event that the Supreme Court of Canada issued such a ruling, it is inconceivable that the court system would become involved in negotiating and endorsing a system of government adapted to the needs and aspirations of the extraordinarily diverse Native collectivites in

Canada. The decision whether or not to endorse one or more types of Native self-government is inescapably a political matter. Of course lawyers can be very perceptive and sensitive in developing moral and political arguments, but when they do so they are no longer employing the legal approach.

The Rights-Based Approach

The rights-based approach invokes, either for or against Native self-government, fundamental moral rights. Proponents of self-government commonly appeal to the natural right either of aboriginal peoples to control their own destiny, or of distinct peoples to national self-determination. Opponents commonly appeal to fundamental rights which, though embodied in law, are thought to be moral as well as legal. Preeminent among the moral rights invoked by opponents of increased Native political self-determination is the right of equality before the law. The typical pattern of reasoning in rights-based arguments is: X (an individual or a group) has a moral right to A. Those who have an obligation to respect X's moral right to A are not doing so or are threatening to stop doing so. Therefore, X's moral right should be made more secure by enacting it as a legal right or, if it is already a legal right, by adhering to it more consistently or enforcing it more strictly.

The rights-based approach does not share the fatal defect of the legal approach, for it does address the crucial question: should there be enacted a legal right of self-government? Moreover, it does not seem possible to make a compelling case that goes to matters of principle, and not just to pragmatic considerations, either for or against increased Native political self-determination, without appealing to moral rights. At the very least, an opponent of Native self-government must maintain that equality before the law is not merely a legal convention but a fundamental principle. Similarly, a proponent of Native self-government must maintain that Native people have a basic right, so far insufficiently recognized, to exercise control over their own destiny.

The rights-based approach has two serious limitations, one of which has to do with the tone of political discourse and the other with its substance. Both of these limitations stem from a fundamental characteristic of rights. One either has or lacks rights, they cannot be possessed in greater or smaller measure. Rights can differ in the degree to which they are respected by the public at large, and in the degree to which they are protected by state officials, but they cannot differ in the degree to which they are possessed. This feature has consequences for the tone of political discourse. Because rights do not admit of degrees, appeals to rights tend in any context of disagreement to elicit outright denials or countervailing appeals to opposed rights.

More importantly, the rights-based approach also has deleterious consequences for the substance of political discourse. Important political innovations have different effects on different people. Most involve shifts of benefits and burdens from some segments of the population to others. Not surprisingly, people affected or likely to be affected by major proposed innovations want to discuss their effects at some length. However, the rights-based approach inhibits such discussion. By its very nature this approach rules out attention to the concrete implications of political innovations for particular individuals and groups. Only implications for the protection of moral rights are to the point. This neglect of the concrete is particularly ill-suited to the issue of Native self-government.

Consider first the problem that confronts anyone who would oppose Native self-government simply on the ground that it conflicts with a moral right of equality before the law. None of the liberal democracies, including Canada, treats this right as absolutely inviolable, and opponents of Native self-government would have a very difficult time making a plausible case based on utterly inflexible application of an abstract right of equality before the law. However, a strictly rights-based defence of Native self-government would be no easier. There are several reasons why this is so, but for present purposes one will suffice. Thoroughly independent, "sovereign," self-governing Native collectivities are not a viable option. No matter what moral rights are possessed by Native persons or collectivities, therefore, the central question that must be addressed pertains to the legal jurisdiction of self-governing Native communities. Which legal rights are to be assigned to these communities, and which are to be retained by the provincial and federal governments? This question cannot be answered by appealing to moral rights. If there are to be self-governing Native collectivities, it must be decided somehow which legal rights it is "fitting" that Native governments should exercise. But "fittingness" cannot be determined solely by appealing to moral rights. Considerations other than moral rights must be invoked to determine how far legal rights should extend.

The Well-Being Approach

The well-being approach sees practices, institutions, policies and so on as better the more they promote, and worse the more they inhibit, the well-being of those who are affected by them. The term "well-being" is not used here in any narrow, utilitarian sense. It is used rather as a "convoy concept,"[5] referring to all the qualities of life that make it better rather than worse. The well-being approach to Native self-government, as long as it does not ignore rights altogether, is superior to the rights-based approach. For one thing, it inhibits the unduly combative tone that is provoked by concentrating on rights; it promotes dialogue, negotiation and compromise, instead of the antagonistic assertion of irreconcilable principles. As well, it encourages attention to the concrete implications of changes in law and policy. Finally, it does not construe the issue of Native political self-determination as an either/or proposition. It encourages attention to questions about the appropriate jurisdiction of Native governments, asking why it is desirable or undesirable that a particular collectivity should exercise a particular power. It rejects the view that there are only two alternatives, either Native self-government or no Native self-government, and the equally untenable view that all self-governing Native collectivities must have the same scope of jurisdiction.

Application of the Well-Being Approach to the Metis Settlements

A perspective that focusses on well-being yields the following broad principle regarding Native political self-determination: Native collectivities should have a legal right of self-government to the extent that recognition of such a right promises to enhance the well-being of such collectivities, without seriously reducing the well-being of Natives who are not members of such collectivities or of non-Natives. This general principle has hardly any practical purchase, since it does not identify any concrete considerations that militate for or against Native self-government. Thus, it is necessary to formulate propositions both for and against increased Native political self-determination in general, and then relate them to the Alberta Metis settlements in particular.

Desire for Increased Autonomy

The greater the support for Native self-government by members of the community for which it is contemplated, the stronger the case for it becomes. In the last chapter the opinions of the respondents at Osprey Lake and Paskwaw about self-government were documented; opinions on both settlements ranged from unqualified support, through indifference, to unqualified opposition. However, the opinions of these respondents suggest that a prudent, gradual and limited movement in the direction of greater political self-determination would be favoured.

Territory

The case for Native self-government is strongest where Native collectivities have a territory within which to exercise their jurisdiction.[6] It is certainly possible to draw the boundaries of political jurisdictions, at least in part, on nonterritorial grounds. This is done when professional associations are granted limited rights to police the conduct of their own members. There may be grounds for granting urban Native collectivities the right to form governments for special purposes—child welfare, medical services, and care for the elderly, for instance—but there must be rather narrow limits to the extent to which residents of the same territory are subject to different laws. When the right of Native self-government is considered, that right must be confined, for the most part, to collectivities that occupy a territory within which that right can be exercised.

The settlements fare very well on this criterion. They have definite territories within which to exercise jurisdiction, and their control of these territories is secure. As a matter of law, Metis settlement lands are not held in fee simple, but there is no prospect that the borders of the settlements will be altered without the settlers' consent. In fact, negotiations currently underway will almost certainly solidify the security of settlement land.

Political Health

The case for Native self-government is strengthened if the community for which it is proposed is politically healthy. There are many dimensions to political health. Here reference is made only to the dimension discussed in the last chapter—a combination of open expression of political conflicts and an underlying consensus strong and inclusive enough that conflicts are manageable in ways compatible with democratic norms—leaving others for discussion below. A community that is either politically apathetic or driven by unbridgeable political schisms is not a good candidate for increased autonomy.

As seen in the last chapter, the settlements studied score quite well on the dimension of political health. On balance, the "rank-and-file" residents of these communities exhibit an impressive level of political awareness, participation and willingness to air their opinions. It is reasonable to suppose that their major shortcoming—lack of familiarity and concern with the FMSA—would be ameliorated under a regime of increased political self-determination.

Political and Administrative Skills

Well developed political and administrative skills among a community's members also enhance the case for self-government. Even if such skills were not required merely to exercise the internal powers of a rural municipality, they would be necessary to deal with the complex intergovernmental relations in which a self-governing Native community would inescapably become involved. To mention only one important factor, there is no prospect that in the foreseeable future any but a very few Native governments would be able to provide an acceptable level of services from funds generated by members of their own communities. Heavy reliance on funding from senior governments would be unavoidable for years to come, and formidable political skills would be required to ensure that this funding was maintained at an appropriate level.

The settlements seem to deserve marginally acceptable grades on this criterion. Five points are worth mentioning in this connection. First, most councillors are fully capable of handling their duties insofar as they relate to the existing internal affairs of their own settlement. Second, most settlements contain a considerable number of potential councillors capable of performing as well as most incumbents. Third, most of the settlements have a very small group of truly outstanding politicians; talent at the highest levels is very thin. Fourth, the scarcity of politicians with outstanding skills is more a matter of disposition than of "natural" ability. The principal weakness of most settlement politicians is their unwillingness to do what is necessary to learn how to deal effectively with off-settlement institutions and events. Finally, administrative talent is thin now, but noticeably improving.

Self-Esteem

The argument for greater Native political self-determination becomes more convincing if it is shown that the self-esteem of members of the community in which it is implemented will thereby be enhanced. It has been argued that poor scores by Natives on the usual indicators of well-being are closely associated with low self-esteem, and especially with a sense of powerlessness. It is true that Native people are not strangers either to the sense or to the reality of powerlessness. If a perception of powerlessness is a major factor in the low self-esteem of many Native people, this consideration will almost invariably militate in favour of increased political self-determination.

There are two factors which must be considered when recommending greater political self-determination for the Alberta Metis settlements. The first is that there are two important divisions within the settlements. One is between those who are largely indifferent to politics and those who are deeply engaged politically. The other is between those who see favouritism as a major and persistent problem and those who see it as minor and rapidly diminishing. Those who are politically engaged and unworried about favouritism tend to be resentful of what they regard as unwarranted interference by government in matters that they believe could be handled far more effectively at the local level. There is little doubt that their self-esteem would be enhanced by greater political autonomy. On the other hand, those who are politically indifferent would be likely to remain so, at least in the short run. It is unlikely that increased political self-determination would affect their self-esteem. Finally, those who see favouritism as a major problem might well suffer a decrease in self-esteem, believing that existing differences in status would be reinforced or even intensified if they were recognized in law as well as in practice.

The second factor is that the probable consequences of increased political self-determination for the self-esteem of settlers cannot be assessed by attending only to short-term effects. Greater autonomy could result in a net increase in self-esteem in the short run but a net decrease in the long run, or vice versa. Sufficient data are not available to make a definite prediction about the long-term effects, but it would appear likely that those who are politically engaged would experience an enhancement of self-esteem not only in the short term but also, and increasingly, as time passes. Second, it is probable that greater political autonomy would gradually diminish the ranks of the politically apathetic but would not eliminate them; increased self-government would have little or no impact on the self-esteem of a sizeable group of settlers. Finally, increased political self-determination would likely reduce the number of settlers who see favouritism as a major problem. Thus, increased political self-determination would likely result in a discernible increase in self-esteem on the settlements. It should be emphasized that this is a conjecture, which depends heavily on the belief that favouritism is declining and would continue to decline under conditions of greater political autonomy. Enough has been said already to indicate that this belief is contestable.

Identification of Problems

The members of a Native collectivity are better equipped than outsiders to identify the nature and causes of many of their problems, and it is in this respect that the case for Native self-government is strongest. The most glaring problems confronting the settlements, especially those that are sometimes experienced by non-Native communities—unemployment, housing shortages, insufficient policing, and so on—are as easily visible to an attentive outsider as to a resident. Additional problems on some settlements, such as schooling, alcohol and drug abuse, and difficulties in providing collateral for loans, are discernible without much additional effort. However, there are some problems taken very seriously by the Metis that seem not to be grasped readily by government officials. Such problems tend to centre on matters in regard to which the Metis have distinctive outlooks and aspirations that are not easily appreciated by outsiders. For example, government officials seem to have had more than a little difficulty in comprehending the unease of the settlers regarding their legal title to their lands. From the viewpoint of the officials, it is obvious that settlement lands are perfectly secure in practice, but the settlers remember that in the early days two settlements were closed down without consultation, and settlers will remain nervous until their lands are legally secured. Government officials have also had difficulty seeing why the Metis leave so much settlement land "lying in waste." Occasionally they have become incensed when settlements with large tracts of unoccupied land have imposed membership freezes. But from the viewpoint of the Metis, "wasteland" is essential to the maintenance of their way of life, which requires unoccupied land not only for the traditional pursuits of hunting, trapping, fishing and gathering, but also for retreats from settled life. Finally, government officials have had some difficulty in grasping the political importance the Metis wish to assign to their elders. In the view of most Metis, elders should be assigned a formal role in settlement government as respected and effective advisors regarding intractable disagreements.

As far as identification of problems is concerned, then, the situation suggests the desirability of divided jurisdiction. There are a number of respects in which the problems that confront the Metis settlements are similar to those faced by other communities, and in those respects there is no case for increased political autonomy for the settlements. However, in other respects, especially those that are culture-specific, the case for increased political self-determination is persuasive.

Solution of Problems

Just as there are many cases in which Native collectivities are more adept than outsiders at identifying problems, so too they are often better equipped than outsiders to deal effectively with the problems that confront them. When the members of the collectivity are better able both to identify the roots of the problem and to devise an effective solution, the case for lodging authority to make policy in the community is strengthened.

Although unemployment, which was identified by the settlers themselves as the principal problem facing them, must remain primarily a federal and provincial government concern, the settlements do appear to have a role to play in creating wage-paying jobs. For one thing, there is certainly room for entrepreneurship on the settlements, through the establishment of orthodox capitalistic, cooperative and settlement-run enterprises. There have already been some successes in this realm, and it is possible that greater political autonomy would encourage more; it seems likely that settlement decision makers would be better able than outsiders to devise policies and programs that would prepare residents of the settlements to participate effectively in the wage economy. The preservation of the conditions essential to the viability of the traditional economy would also seem to require cooperation between settlement governments and the provincial government, with the former possessing both greater expertise and a larger stake in the success of management programs. This suggests increased, but not exclusive, jurisdiction for the settlements. It would be a mistake, of course, to suppose that unemployment is the only important problem on the settlements. There are others in regard to which members of the settlements are more likely than outsiders to devise and implement effective policies. The areas of child welfare, care for the elderly, some aspects of education, and some aspects of health care come quickly to mind.

As in the realm of identifying problems, so in the realm of solving them no absolute case for or against self-government by the settlements seems to emerge. In both realms there appears to be a case for increased settlement self-determination but no case for a wholesale supplanting of provincial jurisdiction.

Economic Independence

There is no prospect that in the foreseeable future the settlements, or any other self-governing Native collectivites, will be able to support themselves on finances generated by their own memberships. If increased political self-determination enhances well-being significantly in ways already discussed, Metis settlers will become increasingly self-confident, self-respectful and better skilled and hence increasingly employable in better-paying jobs. They will thus be better able to contribute to the financing of services provided to their communities. Moreover, they will be better equipped to solve their own problems and thereby less of a burden on the government treasury. Nevertheless, even under the most optimistic scenarios, the settlements will be heavily dependent on governmental financial assistance for a long time. Without such assistance discussion of increased self-government is simply an exercise of imagination. If there is a case on grounds of well-being for greater political autonomy for the settlements, there is thereby a case on grounds of well-being for provision by governments of guaranteed, unconditional grants to the settlements to make the increased autonomy workable.

Representativeness of Leaders

The final consideration in regard to the desirability of increased political autonomy for the Native collectivities could be seen as another dimension of "political health." The more representative the leaders are of their "rank-and-file" members, the stronger the case for self-government. However, while it is generally understood that one "thing" represents another if it somehow "stands for" the other, there are many ways in which one thing can stand for another. Students of representation have identified a number of ways in which a political representative can stand for his or her constituents. Moreover, there is a good deal of disagreement about the relative importance of various types, forms or dimensions of political representation.[7] Only one aspect of this debate will be examined here: to what extent do the views of the elected politicians correspond to those of their constituents? If a political leader deviates markedly from the views of his or her constituents in regard to a matter on which a substantial majority of the latter hold a strong and reasonably well-considered view, the leader is defective in political representativeness. The more frequently deviations of this sort occur within a Native collectivity, the weaker its case for greater political self-determination.

How do the Metis settlements fare in relation to this criterion? The evidence available to us relates to the views of the councillors and their constituents at Paskwaw and Osprey Lake. Only three issues were found on which a substantial majority of the respondents had a reasonably well-considered opinion. First, a substantial majority of the respondents on both settlements, though favourably disposed towards the RCMP, believed that they were underpoliced. Second, a large majority on both settlements held that favouritism was a serious problem. Finally, an overwhelming majority on each settlement held that unemployment was by far the most important issue faced by the settlement. Did the settlement councillors mirror the views of their constituents? As regards the RCMP, at Osprey Lake one of the councillors had no opinion, one regarded the force as unequivocally excellent, and the other three reflected the predominant view of the respondents that the community was underpoliced. At Paskwaw, one councillor had no opinion and the other four shared the view of the vast majority of their constituents that they suffered from inadequate police protection. At Osprey Lake two of the councillors saw favouritism as a genuine but comparatively small problem, and the other three saw it as a very minor concern. At Paskwaw, two of the councillors saw it as a serious matter of concern, and the other three saw it as a minor problem, occurring only in a few, isolated cases. Concerning unemployment, one of the councillors at Osprey Lake saw it as the settlement's second-largest problem, one saw it as a problem though not one of the two most serious, and three did not mention it as a problem at all. At Paskwaw, two of the councillors saw unemployment as the settlement's most serious problem, one saw it as the second-largest problem, and two did not mention it.

On the dimension of representativeness considered here, the record of the Metis councillors, at least on the two settlements studied, must be considered spotty. Although there was fairly close correspondence between the opinions of representatives and those represented regarding policing, on the matters of favouritism and unemployment, there was a noticeable divergence, especially at Osprey Lake. In fairness, it should be repeated that only one dimension of the multifaceted practice of representation has been considered here. Nevertheless, it is an important dimension, and the fact that the Metis councillors did not fare very well on it cannot be dismissed lightly.

Implications

An approach to the issue of Native self-government that focusses more than is usual on considerations of well-being and less on moral rights does not yield the kind of sharp, unequivocal conclusions many people desire. As applied to the situation of the Alberta Metis settlements, this approach suggests that some increase in the strength and scope of the jurisdiction of the settlement governments would be likely to bring about a significant increase in the well-being of the settlers. Moreover, no serious reduction in the well-being of others seems to be threatened by such a move towards greater autonomy. However, the well-being approach does not suggest that a massive shift of authority to the settlements is called for. There are important respects in which the Metis settlers are distinctive and are likely to be able to clarify and satisfy their aspirations, as well as identify and solve their problems, better than outsiders could. But there are also important respects in which the conditions of their well-being are not significantly different from those of their non-Native neighbours. The solution seems clear: increased political self-determination in some spheres but not in others.[8] The practical implication of this conclusion is also clear: Metis and government leaders should pursue consultations and negotiations to specify the nature and scope of the jurisdictional rights of the settlements. While the principal emphasis of such discussions should be on considerations of well-being, it should be kept in mind that the well-being approach does not ignore rights, it only decries over-emphasis of them. Accordingly, discussions leading to the definition of the legal rights of the settlements should not be treated as exercises in social work. Representatives of the provincial government should recognize that they have both a legal and a moral obligation to consult and negotiate with the Metis representatives. Fortunately, respect for rights, as well as concern for well-being, is the stated position of both government and Metis leaders. Consultations and negotiations have already gone some distance, a process which will be examined in the next chapter.

NOTES

1. For example, in the Dene Declaration it is asserted that "the Government of Canada is not the government of the Dene. The Government of the Northwest Territories is not the Government of the Dene. These governments were not the choice of the Dene, they were imposed upon the Dene." Quoted in Michael Asch, *Home and Native Land* (Toronto: Methuen, 1984), 128. Fred Plain, former president of the Union of Ontario Indians, maintains that "The criteria for recognition as a nation are: that the people have a permanent population; that they have a defined territory; that they have a government; that they have the ability to enter into relations with other states. We can assure Canada and the international community that using these criteria we can define ourselves as a nation." Fred Plain, "A Treatise on the Rights of the Aboriginal Peoples of North America," in M. Boldt and J. Anthony Long, eds., *The Quest for Justice: Aboriginal Peoples and Aboriginal Rights* (Toronto: University of Toronto Press, 1984), 35.
2. See, for example, Alberta Federation of Metis Settlement Associations, *Metisism: A Canadian Identity* (Edmonton: n.p., 1982), Chapter 2.
3. See, for example, Brian Slattery, "The Hidden Constitution: Aboriginal Rights in Canada," In Boldt and Long, *The Quest for Justice*, 114-38.
4. Asch, *Home and Native Land*, 52-53.
5. The term "convoy concept" is borrowed from David Braybrooke's *Three Tests for Democracy: Personal Rights, Human Welfare, Collective Preference* (New York: Random House, 1968), 92.

6. Of course this does not mean "where they already have a territory." There can be grounds of well-being (and also of right) for the creation of additional territories.
7. See Hannah F. Pitkin, *The Concept of Representation* (Berkeley: University of California Press, 1972), for a superb discussion of the nature and problems of representation. A briefer discussion can be found in J. Paul Johnston, "Representation," in T.C. Pocklington, ed., *Liberal Democracy in Canada and the United States* (Toronto: Holt, Rinehart and Winston, 1985), Chapter 4.
8. A thoughtful, rich, carefully researched treatment of the implementation of Native government is Frank Cassidy and Robert L. Bish, *Indian Government: Its Meaning in Practice* (Lantzville, B.C.: Oolichan Books, 1989). This book confines its attention to the development, prospects, and problems of the government of communities of status Indians. However, many of its findings are relevant to the Metis. Moreover, it is particularly valuable because its treatment of practical problems is fuller and more detailed than that provided in this chapter.

10

Conferences and Negotiations

The principal purpose of this chapter is to examine the discussions and negotiations concerning land and self-government between the provincial government, the settlements and the FMSA since 1984. Of course the Metis yearning for security of land and greater political self-determination long predates the formation of the Alberta Metis settlements, but our concern here is with major political developments, and for this reason we begin our discussion with the formation of the FMSA in 1975. It was only at this point that there began a concerted, organized effort to guarantee the integrity of settlement lands and, to a much lesser extent, to expand the political autonomy of the settlements.

The FMSA was formed with both a general and a specific purpose in mind. The general purpose was to facilitate cooperation among the settlements, and the specific purpose was to induce the provincial government—by negotiation if possible but by litigation if necessary—to put the revenues derived from the sale of subsurface resources into the Metis Population Betterment Trust Account. Negotiation was abandoned in favour of litigation, which is still before the courts. In 1977, the provincial government and the settlements agreed that there should be no change to the Metis Betterment Act as long as the litigation proceeded. There was a good test of this agreement in 1980, when there was a general consolidation, with some revisions, of the whole body of Alberta statutes. In the course of this consolidation, the Metis Betterment Act was revised to include a new definition of settlement land as "public land allocated for occupation by a settlement association." The Metis saw this wording as definitely prejudicial to their case, since it suggested that the government simply found it expedient to allocate some public land to the settlements. Accordingly, the FMSA quickly arranged a meeting with the premier and reminded him of the "no change" agreement. The result was that the commitment was honoured: the offending statute was repealed and the earlier version restored.

Important developments in regard both to land and to political self-determination resulted from the raids on the settlement offices in 1979. The ensuing investigation by the Alberta ombudsman led to the formation of the MacEwan Committee (see Chapter 5). The committee's report, presented in 1984, was one of the most important documents of the 1970s and 1980s in the of recognition of Metis rights to land and political self-determination. However, it recognized the importance of another document, which had been prepared by the FMSA in 1982 for the constitutional conferences.

The Essay on Metisism

In June 1982 the FMSA published a sixty-five-page booklet entitled *Metisism: A Canadian Identity,* billed as its "Statement on Aboriginal Rights in the Constitution of Canada." *Metisism* was addressed to Premier Lougheed by the then president of the FMSA. It was described as the FMSA's submission on matters concerning the position of aboriginal peoples to be addressed at the constitutional conference. However, the booklet was intended for a much wider audience than the premier and his advisors. *Metisism* does not read like a pamphlet intended only for short-term use, but like a declaration that is meant to retain currency for several years at least. Although the booklet is not organized on this basis, it makes three kinds of appeals: philosophical, legal, and political.

The philosophical claims in *Metisism* state the nature and justification of Metis aboriginal rights, especially to land and special political status. "Quite simply," the document asserts, "aboriginal rights are the collective rights of aboriginal peoples."[1] There is no argument to defend the thesis that anyone, aboriginal or not, has collective rights. Nor is there any argument in support of the view that all the collective rights of aboriginal peoples are aboriginal rights; these fundamental theses are taken for granted. The apparent justifications of the claims of Metis aboriginal rights are presented with similar brevity. First, it is asserted that "the Metis had developed as a distinctive people. Together with the Indian tribes, they controlled the North-West. The reality of Metis economic, social and political organization could not be ignored by Canada."[2] This argument is most unclear. Does it assert that "Canada" could not have ignored, or would have been unwise to ignore, the physical might of the Metis? If so, it is hard to see how it establishes any kind of right. It is also hard to see how an argument based on either numbers or strength could be helpful to a group that is now relatively weak in both respects. The second defence of Metis aboriginal rights is that "the Metis had aboriginal rights because of their Indian ancestry."³ This claim is not obvious. Assuming that Indians do have aboriginal rights because of their aboriginal status, it is not obvious that such rights devolve upon people who are not aboriginal. Of course, this is not to say that no philosophical case for Metis aboriginal rights can be made. However, there was no serious effort to make such a case in *Metisism*.

The booklet contains a clever legal argument in support of the settlers' rights to settlement lands, which begins with the proposition that there are only two possible views of the Metis settlements. In the first view, which "involves traditional white paternalism,"⁴ the settlements were simply a Depression welfare scheme that bore no relationship to earlier Metis claims, so that while the settlers were permitted to use settlement land, they had no legal interest or title in it. The alternative, a "traditional native view," saw the settlements, like Indian reserves, as a partial recognition of historic aboriginal rights. In this view, the government "holds the formal title to the land, but simply as a trustee," the residents of the settlements, like residents of Indian reserves, hold the "usufructuary" interest in their lands. That is, they are actually entitled to the beneficial use of it. In *Metisism*, it is argued that this usufructuary right, which has been recognized generally by the courts as pertaining to Indian reserve lands, must be applied also to settlement lands, for the only alternative would be "a crude paternalism which would make native interests permanently subject to the whims of government."⁵ This argument is not conclusive, but it is imaginative and packs a good deal of rhetorical punch. In this respect it is as much political as legal.

Metisism deals with two kinds of political concerns—governmental arrangements, and those public policies deemed important to the cultural and economic viability of the settlements. Both the tone and the content of the booklet's position on governmental arrangements are expressed in the observation that "we seek a distinct, not a separate, political status within Canadian federalism."⁶ The emphasis throughout the discussion of the political status of the settlements is that they should come under the political jurisdiction of the province, except in regard to the protection of aboriginal rights: "we cannot trust the province to serve as the ultimate guarantor of our rights [so that] we are prepared to accept provincial jurisdiction over the Metis Settlements except in matters relating to our aboriginal rights."⁷ This position requires some explanation. First, in the absence of a reasonably definite statement of the scope of Metis aboriginal rights, it is not enlightening about the demarcation between federal and provincial jurisdiction. Second, the record of the federal government in dealing with the Metis hardly gives grounds for confidence that it would be a vigilant defender of their rights. However, it must be said that these remarks make a great deal of sense as an exercise in political strategy and tactics. By forswearing any aspiration to "sovereignty," *Metisism* underscores the reasonableness and realism of its authors. Furthermore, by pledging qualified allegiance to both the provincial and federal governments, it keeps open options for negotiations with both.

The booklet supports a constitutional guarantee of aboriginal representation both in the House of Commons and in the provincial legislatures. Further proposed is a distinct provincial constituency composed of the Metis settlements.[8] Oddly, the document has little to say about local government. A section entitled "Local Self-government and Taxation" is concerned almost exclusively with exempting the settlements from any but self-imposed property taxation.

Metisism has a good deal to say about public policies deemed important to the cultural and economic well-being of the settlements. A matter that is clearly seen as significant both culturally and politically is eligibility for membership in a settlement association. Metis politicians seem to be agreed on two points: that only Metis have a right to decide who Metis are, and that a definition of Metis should not be restrictively racial. The following statement is typical:

> We are opposed to the use of narrow racial criteria to define Metis people; literal interpretation of the [Metis Betterment] Act's definition would exclude even Louis Riel from membership in a Metis Settlement Association. We accept as Metis any person of mixed Indian and non-Indian ancestry who identifies as Metis.[9]

The booklet states a number of concerns about the maintenance and enhancement of Metis culture. Grave concerns are expressed about the schooling received by settlement children. Among the reforms proposed are guaranteed Metis representation on school boards in areas with large Metis populations, more attention to Metis history and culture in those areas, and teaching of the Cree language in areas where numbers warrant.

The final claim in *Metisism* is that the settlement areas are economically viable. Several points are made in this connection, the most interesting of which has to do with regional disparities and programs to reduce them. The authors suggest that a federal and provincial commitment to reduce economic disparities between aboriginal peoples and other Canadians and to reduce disparities between northern and southern regions would measurably increase the economic prospects of the settlements.

The MacEwan Report

The principal concern of the MacEwan Report was to present recommendations for a new act to govern the Metis settlements. Although the committee members acknowledged that their work would require some revisions, the report contained a nearly complete draft of a new act. The specific recommendations for new legislation were preceded by a two-page section in which the committee stated the general thrust of its proposals. This discussion is summarized in the following sentence: "The Committee believes that its recommendations provide a framework for dealing with the paramount concerns of local self-government and land security."[10]

The main thrust of the MacEwan Report was examined in Chapter 5, but of interest here is its statement of principles:

> (1) the Metis represent a unique cultural group in Canada, an aboriginal people recognized in the Canadian Constitution, and a group that has played a major role in the development of Western Canada;
>
> (2) because the culture and lifestyle of the Metis Settlements is inextricably linked to the land, a Metis Settlement land base is the cornerstone on which to build and maintain the social, cultural and economic strength of the Metis settlers;
>
> (3) given a unique culture and the land base of the Metis Settlement Areas, the Metis can best achieve the mutual goal of self-reliant integration, without homogenization, by a legislative framework enabling the maximum practicable local self-government of the land base;
>
> (4) it would not be possible to include in Metis settlement local government the full scope of powers required to deal with all matters of health, education, social services and economic development, but even in these cases the uniqueness of the culture and its problem solving traditions should be respected by the Government bodies exercising the power.[11]

The MacEwan Report combines a reasonably clear statement of fundamental principles with an effort to express those principles in workable legislation. Subsequent efforts do not depart significantly from the work of the MacEwan Committee. The basic principles remain the same, and proposed legislation does not deviate substantially from the form it was given in this first major Metis-government effort.

Development of a "Made in Alberta" Approach

In 1985, at the second of the First Ministers' Conferences on constitutional matters affecting Native people, Premier Lougheed, along with Premier Bennett of British Columbia, strongly opposed the constitutional entrenchment of any aboriginal rights that were not given clear definitions. Lougheed was portrayed by some journalists as unsympathetic to Native people. Possibly stung by this sort of criticism, he was receptive to an FMSA proposal to take concrete steps towards the legal recognition of specific rights of some Alberta Natives.

FMSA Proposal and Initial Government Response

In brief, the proposal was that the Alberta Act, which is part of the Canadian Constitution, should be amended so as to recognize the settlements' title to their lands. Advisors of the premier urged that, before precipitous steps were taken to secure a constitutional amendment, the settlements should be required to perform two tasks. First, they should define fair and democratic criteria for membership in settlement associations. Second, they should state fair and democratic standards for the allocation of settlement lands. The imposition of these two preconditions was suggested both by considerations of principle and by considerations of political prudence. As a matter of principle, all Metis have a legitimate interest in the conditions for membership in the settlements. And as a matter of political prudence, the MAA occasionally charged that the settlements were run exclusively for the benefit of a privileged few, without concern for the vast majority of Alberta Metis who were not, and had little prospect of becoming under existing policy, members of settlement associations. It was agreed that the settlements should come up with fair and democratic criteria for membership and land allocation before the government would take further steps towards constitutional entrenchment.

The Westlock Resolution

The settlements moved quickly to comply with the government's conditions. At an all-council meeting in Westlock, Alberta in late April 1985, principles to govern the granting of membership and the allocation of land were agreed upon. The main provisions of the so-called Westlock Resolution were:

> The definition of "Metis" would be the one first intimated in *Metisism* and then refined in the *MacEwan Report* (aboriginal ancestry plus identification with Metis history and culture).

Applications for membership in a Metis Settlement would be considered by the Settlement Council and would be granted under due process subject to: an Alberta residency requirement; the availability of suitable land; the ability and willingness of the applicant to use the land allotted to him/her effectively and to adhere to the by-laws of the Settlement.

On approval of membership and improvement of land allocated to him/her in accordance with the by-laws of the Settlement, the member would acquire the highest form of ownership of Settlement land, namely, a Certificate of Occupancy.

There would be a right of appeal on all matters affecting land and membership rights to "a lawfully constituted body of Metis people consisting in the most part of Settlement Elders."

The resolution concludes with a commitment of the FMSA board that "the Metis Settlements continue to work with the Government of the Province of Alberta to complete and implement the recommendations of the [MacEwan] Committee and the principles of this Resolution."

Resolution 18

The Westlock Resolution satisfied the government's conditions for moving forward on constitutional entrenchment of settlement land rights. After consultation with senior elected officials and civil servants, on 3 June 1985 Premier Lougheed moved Resolution 18 in the Legislative Assembly. The preamble commits the government to take certain steps. For one thing, it specifically mentions constitutional entrenchment through amendment of the Alberta Act. For another, it implicitly endorses increased political self-determination for the settlements by asserting that "if enlarged jurisdiction is to be achieved, Metis people have the responsibility to determine distinctive methods and institutions for such management and governance."[12] Finally, by specifically mentioning the work of the MacEwan Committee, the government commits itself to the fundamental principles and general recommendations agreed upon by that committee.

The resolution specifies that the government of Alberta will grant existing Metis settlement lands to the settlement associations or other appropriate corporate bodies "to be held on behalf of the Metis people of Alberta." It further endorses the grant of these lands in fee simple, reserving thereout all mines and minerals but without prejudice to existing litigation; the grant is made subject to the continuing legislative authority of the province. The resolution provides that "as a first step toward the grant of existing Metis settlement lands, it is the responsibility of the Metis to define and propose: (a) fair and democratic criteria for membership in settlement associations and for settlement lands allocation to individual members of settlement associations; and (b) the composition of democratic governing bodies for the management and governance of Metis Settlements," and commits the government to introduce a revised Metis Betterment Act once this has been completed. Finally, it commits the government to seek, once a revised Metis Betterment Act has been enacted, a constitutional amendment granting the settlements fee simple title to the settlement lands.

Resolution 18, which was adopted unanimously by the legislature, put the ball back in the FMSA's court. A literal reading of the resolution might suggest that only one task remained for the FMSA: to propose "the composition of democratic governing bodies for the management and governance of Metis Settlements," since the responsibilities in regard to land and membership had already been handled in the Westlock Resolution. In fact, however, there was a great deal more work to do. For the Metis politicians would have been most unwise, even if they had been inclined, to leave the drafting of a new act to the government.

The Early Response to Resolution 18

The FMSA's immediate reaction to Resolution 18 was to strike a Task Force to determine how to respond to it. The Task Force was composed of experienced members of the executive and board of the FMSA and other respected settlement politicians. In the fall of 1985, the Task Force toured the settlements, seeking opinions on membership, land allocation and governing bodies; it reported to the FMSA board. In the spring of 1986 a former president of the FMSA and a Native Studies scholar from one of the Alberta universities were hired to put together an official settlements response to Resolution 18.

Meanwhile, another committee was struck to consider the response to Resolution 18. Known as the "Core Group," this committee, unlike the Task Force, consisted of government as well as settlement members. Its members were the then president and vice-president of the FMSA, the director of the MDB, and the ADM to whom the MDB reported. Attached to the Core Group were a lawyer from the FMSA and a lawyer from Municipal Affairs, who were to play an important part in constructing a response to Resolution 18. The Core Group was able to anticipate to some extent the likely responses of elected officials and senior civil servants.

"By Means of Conferences and Negotiations"

In July 1986 the FMSA published a seventy-six-page booklet entitled *"By Means of Conferences and Negotiations" We Ensure Our Rights:*

Background and Principles for New Legislation Linking Metis Aboriginal Rights to "A Resolution Concerning an Amendment to the Alberta Act" (*BMOC*). *BMOC* was addressed to Premier Getty by the FMSA board and was designed in particular to meet the responsibility assigned by the legislature to the Metis in Resolution 18 (see above). It added little of importance to the Westlock Resolution, and all the changes introduced by *BMOC* in regard to membership and land had to do with the bodies that hear appeals from settlement council decisions. The interesting innovations proposed in *BMOC* had to do with the composition of governing bodies for the Metis settlements.

BMOC proposed four types of bodies, each with its own role to play in settlement government: elected settlement councils; appointed elders committees; Metis arbitration tribunals; and an elected Metis settlement *okimawiwin* (governing council, from a Cree word for government). The respective roles of these bodies are stated briefly in *BMOC*:

> The Settlement Councils and Elders Committees are permanent institutions functioning on each settlement. The Metis arbitration tribunals are ad hoc conflict resolution bodies created in a manner similar to arbitration boards under the Alberta *Arbitration Act.* The Metis Okimawiwin is a central body consisting of all settlement councils and representing the settlements overall. It provides a basis in legislation for recognizing the system that has been functioning effectively for the settlements since 1980.[13]

With one exception, all the *BMOC* provisions relating to the powers and responsibilities of settlement councils complied with what had been accepted in several earlier documents. The exception was a new proposal that "bylaws and resolutions shall be consistent with the policies of *okimawiwin* and shall be void to the extent of any inconsistency with those policies."[14]

There was a considerable difference between the elders committees and the senates of elders that had been agreed upon earlier. The nature of the elders groups, as bodies of appeal for controversial decisions regarding membership and allocations of land, were not changed. However, their authority was weakened in two ways. First, instead of being elected as senates of elders as proposed earlier, the elders committees would be appointed by the various settlement councils.[15] Second, any dispute not resolvable by an elders committee could be appealed to a Metis arbitration tribunal.[16]

BMOC portrays Metis arbitration tribunals as final courts of appeal in disputes concerning membership and land, whether the disputants be settlements, members of settlements, applicants for membership, settlement councils, or *okimawiwin*. If agreed by the disputants, a Metis arbitration tribunal may consist of a single person. However, BMOC leaves open the possibility that each party to a dispute could choose one or two members of a tribunal, and that they would subsequently choose another person as chairman.[17] Provision is made for the award of a tribunal to have the force of a court order.[18]

Without doubt, the major innovation of BMOC was the proposal to create a Metis settlements *okimawiwin*. BMOC proposes the creation of *okimawiwin* as a corporate body composed very much like the current FMSA. The supreme legislative authority in *okimawiwin* would be lodged in its general council, which would consist of the members of all settlement councils plus a president, vice-president, secretary and treasurer, who would be selected as those officers are now selected for the FMSA. The policies of *okimawiwin* would be established by its general council, but the management of its affairs would be assigned to an executive council, consisting of the executive officers plus the chairmen of the various settlement councils. Thus, the executive council of *okimawiwin* would have the same membership as the board of directors of the FMSA. The powers of *okimawiwin* would be very extensive under the BMOC proposal. For one thing, the fee simple title to all settlement lands would be vested in *okimawiwin* rather than the individual settlements. For another, *okimawiwin* would be responsible for appointing a registrar of Metis titles, who would be responsible for maintaining a registry of lands and interests in lands of the settlements. Again, a necessary condition for the creation of a new settlement is that it be supported by *okimawiwin*. Also, *okimawiwin* would administer a new Metis Settlements Resources Trust Fund, which would replace the Metis Population Betterment Trust Fund, absorbing the latter's assets. However, most important of all is the proposed authority of *okimawiwin* to make policies, the significance of which is suggested by the following: "Subject to the policies established by *okimawiwin*, a settlement council may make bylaws" on a specified range of quite important matters.[19]

BMOC contained a draft of a new Metis Settlements Act which embodied all three of the requirements stated in Resolution 18: fair and democratic criteria for membership on settlements; fair and democratic criteria for land allocation on settlements; and democratic governing bodies for management and governance of the land. It also contained a proposed amendment to the Alberta Act. FMSA officials therefore expected the province to accept the recommendations in BMOC quickly and with relatively minor reservations. They were to be disappointed.

The Faltering of the "Made in Alberta" Approach

In the late summer of 1986, the premier of Alberta and the president of the FMSA set March 1987 as the target date for a joint announcement that all the conditions had been met for constitutional entrenchment of the settlements' land rights. In early 1987 the concerns of senior officials in the Department of the Attorney General about the possible implications of the proposed legislation and constitutional amendment deepened. The department had a number of worries, but it was especially concerned that the settlements' insistence on "territorial integrity" (whereby the settlements would own the beds and shores of lakes, as well as roads and road allowances) would, if recognized in law, prejudice the province's chance of winning the lawsuit over natural resources. The dispute about territorial integrity slowed discussion of other matters. Finally, the end of 1987 was set as the new target date for agreement on a complete package that was to contain the issuance of letters patent transferring title to the settlement lands to the settlements, an amendment to the Alberta Act and thereby the Canadian Constitution giving the settlement lands constitutional protection, and agreement on the wording of a new Metis Settlement Act.

Soon thereafter senior officials of several departments of the provincial government and officials and employees of the FMSA carried on earnest discussions regarding the implementation of Resolution 18. By early June 1987, a document was available which represented a consensus between FMSA and government officials as to the three elements in the package. On 13 June an all-council meeting voted to approve the document for tabling in the legislature but, specified that two workshops had to be held on each settlement to explain, discuss and review it.

On 17 June 1987, the minister tabled in the Legislative Assembly a document entitled *Implementation of Resolution 18 (A Resolution Concerning an Amendment to the Alberta Act)* (*IR18*). This document consists of proposed drafts of letters patent to transfer title to settlement lands to the settlements, a proposed Alberta Act amendment, and a proposed Metis Settlement Act. *IR18* is noteworthy only for its clarity, precision and neatness: it provides drafts of letters patent and an amendment to the Alberta Act in proper legalese, and it organizes the proposed new Metis Settlements Act in careful language and sets out its provisions in easily intelligible order. Substantively it does not alter proposals set out in *BMOC*. However, unlike *BMOC*, *IR18* makes no provision for senates of elders. Nothing in the proposed legislation prohibits the creation of senates as advisory bodies, but the proposed legislative route of appeal is to the Metis Appeals Tribunal.

At the workshops held on each settlement to discuss *IR18*, the proposals contained in that document met with opposition. One school of thought held that *IR18*, and the FMSA's position generally, were far too weak. According to these critics, *IR18* was a sell-out of the interests of Alberta Metis, in that it did not guarantee significant rights to off-settlement Metis. Some went further and maintained that, by concentrating so heavily on a "made in Alberta" approach, as distinguished from an approach based on Metis aboriginal rights, it ignored the rights and aspirations of Metis in other provinces.

A far more common and vociferous complaint was that *IR18* would give too much power to the settlement councils, to the *okimawiwin*, or both. *IR18*, like BMOC before it, would create in *okimawiwin* an agency with significantly more power than the FMSA, even though it would be a creature of the settlement councils. Some critics claimed to find dictatorial connotations in the very word "okimawiwin." Without getting into the arcane disputes about that issue, let it simply be stated that "Metis Settlements *okimawiwin*" was replaced by "Metis Settlements General Council." Controversy was not merely terminological, however. Some critics were deeply concerned that council bylaws could be invalid if they conflicted with *okimawiwin* policies. The other complaint was that the *IR18* proposals allow, although they do not require, settlement councils to increase the scope of their jurisdiction. As seen in Chapter 8, many settlers are aggrieved by the real or apparent partiality exercised by councillors on behalf of favoured individuals or families. It is not surprising that such settlers were deeply alarmed by the prospect that the jurisdiction of settlement councils could be significantly increased under a new Metis Settlements Act.

IR18 thus became a lightning rod, drawing the wrath both of those who found the FMSA's position too weak and those who found it too strong. However, *IR18* was also attacked from other quarters. In the fall of 1987, some members of one of the eastern settlements who were unhappy with the day-to-day operations of their council struck upon *IR18* as a focus for their concern, and the Metis Coalition Society of Alberta was born. This group was not exclusively preoccupied with the settlements. Its purpose was to act as a watchdog over any group that purported to speak for the Metis people of Alberta. During late 1987 and early 1988, the coalition became a rallying organization for residents of the eastern settlements who, for a variety of reasons, were dissatisfied with their settlement councils or with the FMSA. Since the coalition was not a homogeneous group with an exclusive ideology, it was able to present a wide range of objections to *IR18*. It did so very effectively, much to the delight of both settlers and government officials who were unhappy either with some or all of the the *IR18* proposals, or with the speed with which they were moving towards enactment into law. It was partly because of the effectiveness of coalition opposition that the revised target date for the implementation of Resolution 18 at the end of 1987 was not met.

About-Face: The Victory of the "Made in Alberta" Approach

In light of this opposition, many observers were astonished when, on 21 June 1989, the president of the FMSA and Premier Getty were shown on television warmly shaking hands over an agreement that satisfied the aspirations of most settlers. According to the agreement, settlement land rights and a new system of government would be enshrined in law and, in return for dropping their suit against the government, the settlements would receive about $310 million over seventeen years for capital and operating costs, and to build up a settlement's heritage fund. In this section discussion will focus on the principal events leading up to the surprising breakthrough.

In January 1986, Premier Getty suggested to the then president of the FMSA that it might be advantageous to both sides if the settlements' suit against the government were settled out of court. This suggestion was discussed sporadically for the next couple of years without discernible advance towards agreement. In May 1988, the government increased its pressure. The FMSA received a letter from the provincial attorney general stating unequivocally that none of the commitments in Resolution 18 would be fulfilled until the settlements' suit against the government was settled. Under the leadership of its new president, the board of the FMSA began to discuss the possibility of an out-of-court settlement more urgently and intensively. A consensus was reached that a satisfactory out-of-court settlement was preferable to several more years of legal manoeuvring, especially since new legal advice indicated that there was a real possibility that the case would be lost.

During January and February 1989, agreement was reached. However, fearful that the government might have a change of heart after the upcoming provincial election, the Metis applied some pressure of their own. They threatened to run, just prior to the election, a caravan, complete with wagon trains, from a town northwest of Edmonton (in a constituency which the Conservatives hoped to regain from the Liberals) to the capital (in which the Conservatives hoped to regain some seats from the NDP). The two leaders shook hands on a deal shortly before the election, the premier's commitment contingent on approval of his caucus and the president's contingent on the agreement of the settlement councils. In April, the settlements held an all-council meeting in Jasper. The consensus of the delegates was that the issue was too big to be decided by them without consulting their electorates. Accordingly, a referendum on each settlement, managed by a prestigious accounting firm, was scheduled for 21 June.

These developments did not occur without opposition. The Metis Coalition Society splintered, but out of it there emerged one group, known as Concerned Citizens, which organized resistance. The Concerned Citizens, mainly residents of one western and two eastern settlements, opposed both the agreement itself as defective and the referendum as premature. As to the substance of the proposed agreement, the Concerned Citizens objected to provisions which, in their view, gave too much authority to the settlement councils and the general council. This group was composed mainly of settlers who were particularly wary of the perceived favouritism of settlement institutions, and they wanted legal protection against these practices. As to the referendum, they wanted it postponed until protections were stated precisely and settlers had an opportunity to discuss their adequacy.

More threatening opposition came from Highgrass Plain, the northernmost and most populous settlement. Settlers there went so far as to instruct their council to declare that their settlement would withdraw from the FMSA if a referendum were held. Opposition in Highgrass mirrored that of the Concerned Citizens. A compromise was reached whereby Highgrass would participate in the referendum if a three-day workshop were held, at which officers of the FMSA, government officials and an independent lawyer would explain and answer questions about the proposed agreement. The few Highgrass settlers who attended the workshop eventually endorsed the referendum but urged that, if the agreement were ratified, no legislation should be enacted for six months, so that settlers would have a chance to study and discuss it, and propose clarifications of matters of detail.

The MAA, and especially its president, treated the agreement and the referendum with care. They supported the agreement in principle but expressed reservations about enacting it too quickly. Like the settlers at Highgrass, they called for a six-month period to study the proposed legislation and address some of its details. Not surprisingly, the details that concerned them most were those that dealt with the accessibility of settlement membership to non-settlement Metis.

Both the FMSA and the government were willing to accept the six-month study period. The referendum proceeded as scheduled, and 77 percent of those who voted supported the agreement. The qualification on the FMSA president's acceptance of the agreement—that it had to be supported by the settlements—had been met. The press conference at which the results of the referendum were announced was attended by Premier Getty, who indicated that his party caucus had accepted the agreement; the proviso with which he accepted the agreement was thus also removed. The agreement was to be enacted into law within six months.

The agreement contains six items: 1) The provincial legislature will enact a Metis Settlements Act. Although no doubt there will be some changes in detail, this act will not depart far from the model set out initially in the MacEwan Report and essentially replicated in other documents discussed earlier in this chapter; 2) The legislature will also pass a Metis Settlements Land Act. This act will give the settlements full title to their land; 3) The legislature will pass a resolution calling for an amendment of the Alberta Act whereby the title of settlements to their land will be constitutionally entrenched. Assuming that the federal government complies, no future Alberta government will be able unilaterally to dispossess any settlement of its land; 4) A finances agreement will be struck between the government and the settlements, whereby the settlements will receive (by the end of the agreement) only slightly less than they would have received if their suit had been successful. They will receive $30 million a year for the first seven years of the agreement (1990 to 1997), consisting of $25 million for capital and operating costs and $5 million to be deposited in a heritage fund. According to government officials, if the heritage fund is managed effectively it could be worth $140 million by 2007, when the agreement terminates. Between 1998 and 2007 payments will drop to $10 million a year, which is approximately the amount the settlements would have received under the current system of financing, taking into account inflation and population increases; 5) There will be an agreement for co-management of settlement surface and subsurface resources. Although the settlements will give up their claim to royalties on subsurface resources, they will acquire a voice, with the government, regarding the exploitation of oil and gas. They will no longer come under the jurisdiction of the Surface Rights Act, which currently governs access to, and compensation for, the activities of oil and gas companies on settlement lands; 6) There will be a commission agreement. A commission will be established, selected jointly by the settlements and the government and reporting both to the Metis General Council and the provincial cabinet. The principal area of responsibility of the commission will be financial management and accounting, although it will also be responsible for some spheres of program delivery, mainly housing and transportation. When the commission begins its work, the MDB will be eliminated, its responsibilities assumed by the commission, the settlement councils and the general council. At the end of the initial seven-year period, the commission will be disbanded, and responsibility for governing the settlements will be transferred to the settlement councils and, to a lesser extent, to the general council.

Evidently the Metis settlers have secured an agreement satisfactory to the majority of them, especially in regard to their land claims. However, mindful of a long history of bad faith on the part of Euro-Canadians in regard to promises concerning land, the Metis have wisely refused to drop their suit against the government until the agreement is firmly in place.

NOTES

1. FMSA, *Metisism: A Canadian Identity* (Edmonton: n.p., 1982), "Letter of Transmittal."
2. Ibid., 1.
3. Ibid.
4. Ibid., 57.
5. Ibid., 61.
6. Ibid., 15.
7. Ibid., 19.
8. Ibid., 24-25.
9. Ibid., 31.
10. Government of Alberta, *Report of the MacEwan Joint Metis-Government Committee to Review the Metis Betterment Act and Regulations* (Edmonton: n.p., 1984), 5.
11. Ibid., 59.
12. *Alberta Hansard*, 3 June 1985, p. 1287. All subsequent references to Resolution 18 and Premier Lougheed's comments on it are from this day's *Hansard*, pp. 1287-1291.
13. FMSA, *"By Means of Conferences and Negotiations" We Ensure Our Rights* (Edmonton: n.p., 1986).
14. Ibid., 31.
15. Ibid., 32.
16. Ibid., 48.
17. Ibid., 65-67.
18. Ibid., 69.
19. Ibid., 38.

EPILOGUE

In the Introduction I emphasized that this book was intended to explore a terrain rather than answer a question. The terrain has been explored, so this is neither a summary nor a conclusion. In these last few pages I want to speculate very briefly about the implications for the Metis of the historic 1989 agreement. I consider these implications as they apply first to the Alberta Metis settlements, second as they apply to other rural Metis communities, and finally as they apply to urban Metis.

To the extent that the 1989 agreement was an agreement about title to existing Alberta settlement land, I find it admirable. Not only the substance of the agreement but also the process whereby it was reached bring credit both to the Metis settlers and their representatives and also to the provincial government. In particular, by securing title to the land, the Metis politicians satisfied a fundamental aspiration of the majority of their constituents. In the manner in which they achieved this objective, the Metis politicians displayed a remarkable combination of commitment to principle and political finesse. For its part, the government exhibited an admirable, albeit tardy, willingness to retreat from a legalistic, confrontational posture to one which was more flexible.

The part of the agreement dealing with "self-government" seems to be least satisfactory. Essentially, the self-government provisions of the agreement will transform the Metis settlements into quite conventional rural municipalities. I doubt that these provisions will be sufficient to accommodate the cultural, social and economic uniqueness of the settlements. One should not be surprised if the settlements call for amendments to the new act long before the seventeen-year agreement expires. However, they have given hostages to the future and they will be in for some tough battles.

Another unsatisfactory feature of the agreement is that it makes no provision for the creation of new settlements. It may be that the Alberta government is labouring under the illusion that, at least as far as land is concerned, "the Metis issue" is closed. If so, I think it will be disappointed. Even if the existing settlements do not press for the creation of additional settlements in areas of the province where there are significant concentrations of Metis, it is almost certain that the MAA will make land claims on behalf of the non-settlement Metis. Certainly the MAA will be in a very strong position to argue on grounds of fairness that residents of existing settlements, who constitute a small minority of the province's Metis population, should not be given preferred treatment.

This brings us to our second consideration: the implications of the agreement for rural Metis communities other than the Alberta settlements. The main point here, I believe, is that the Alberta agreement will give new political leverage to such communities. Presumably this leverage will be strongest in the other prairie provinces, but it seems likely to have an effect in Ontario and British Columbia as well. If an Alberta Conservative government with no strong record of concern for Native aspirations, and with its greatest electoral strength concentrated in the southern part of the province where the Metis do not speak with a loud voice, can make an historic agreement, the ability of other provinces to resist similar demands would seem to be seriously reduced. (It would be politically imprudent for any government to suggest that Alberta acted as it did because of the threat imposed by the suit over subsurface resources.) At the very least, the Alberta agreement is bound to strengthen the hands of rural Metis land claimants in other provinces.

Of course, other Metis rural collectivities may be more impressed by the fact of the Alberta agreement than by its terms. For example, some may be attracted to a system of individual title to land, as in the scrip system, rather than the Alberta system of collective ownership. Certainly other Metis groups may seek a more extensive scope of self-government than the one contained in the Alberta agreement. One major effect of the Alberta agreement is likely to be its assistance to other Metis collectivities in deciding what they will and will not seek.

We turn, finally, to a rapidly growing segment of the population, the urban Metis. In my judgement, the Alberta settlements agreement is likely to have little import for Metis committed to urban life, except to the extent that such a major breakthrough may strengthen their morale and determination, while perhaps modestly increasing their bargaining power with municipal and provincial governments. This judgement is based on two main considerations. First, the Alberta settlements agreement is, above all, an agreement about title to land; this is not, to my knowledge, a principal concern of urban Metis political activists. Second, the Alberta agreement, to the extent that it is concerned with greater political autonomy, deals with legal and political considerations that apply to communities with definite territorial boundaries. Of course many urban Native aspirations also require the attainment of increased political self-determination, but in the urban setting increased self-determination means mainly the provision to a unique clientele of new services, the modification of conventional services, or the alteration of the mode of delivery of services. In other words, the basis of demands for increased self-government in urban areas is more functional than territorial. As I see it, then, urban Metis have little to learn from the substance of the Alberta agreement, but I should add that they could do worse than contact the leading politicians of the Alberta Metis settlements for advice about effective negotiation.

SELECTED BIBLIOGRAPHY

Books

Adams, Howard. *Prison of Grass*. Toronto: New Press, 1975.

Asch, Michael. *Home and Native Land: Aboriginal Rights and the Canadian Constitution*. Toronto: Methuen, 1984.

Boldt, Menno and J. Anthony Long, eds. *The Quest for Justice: Aboriginal Peoples and Aboriginal Rights*. Toronto: University of Toronto Press, 1984.

Braybrooke, David. *Three Tests for Democracy: Personal Rights, Human Welfare, Collective Preference*. New York: Random House, 1968.

Campbell, Maria. *Half Breed*. Toronto: McClelland and Stewart, 1973.

Cardinal, Harold. *The Unjust Society*. Edmonton: Hurtig, 1969.

Cardinal, Harold. *The Rebirth of Canada's Indians*. Edmonton: Hurtig, 1977.

Cassidy, Frank and Robert L. Bish. *Indian Government: Its Meaning in Practice*. Lantzville, B.C.: Oolichan Books, 1989.

Cumming, Peter A. and Neil H. Mickenberg, eds. *Native Rights in Canada*. 2nd ed. Toronto: Indian-Eskimo Association of Canada, 1972.

Dahl, Robert A. *A Preface to Democratic Theory*. Chicago: University of Chicago Press, 1956.

Dahl, Robert A. and Edward R. Tufte. *Size and Democracy*. Stanford: Stanford University Press, 1973.

Daniels, Harry W., ed. *The Forgotten People: Metis and Non-Status Indian Land Claims*. Ottawa: Native Council of Canada, 1979.

Dobbin, Murray. *The One-and-a-half Men*. Vancouver: New Star Books, 1981.

Dosman, Edgar. *Indians: The Urban Dilemma*. Toronto: McClelland and Stewart, 1972.

Driben, Paul. *We Are Metis: The Ethnography of a Halfbreed Community in Northern Alberta*. New York: AMS Press, 1985.

Flanagan, Thomas. *Riel and the Rebellion: 1885 Reconsidered*. Saskatoon: Western Producer Prairie Books, 1983.

Frideres, James S. *Native People in Canada: Contemporary Conflicts.* 2nd ed. Toronto: Prentice-Hall, 1983.

Getty, Ian A.L. and Antoine S. Lussier. *As Long as the Sun Shines and Water Flows: A Reader in Canadian Native Studies.* Vancouver: University of British Columbia Press, 1983.

Giraud, Marcel. *The Metis in the Canadian West.* 2 volumes. Edmonton: University of Alberta Press, 1986.

Howard, Joseph K. *The Strange Empire of Louis Riel.* Toronto: Swan Publishing Company, 1952.

Judd, Carol M. and Arthur J. Ray, eds. *Old Trains and New Directions: Papers of the Third North American Fur Trade Conference.* Toronto: University of Toronto Press, 1980.

Mansbridge, Jane J. *Beyond Adversary Democracy.* New York: Basic Books, 1980.

Masson, Jack K. *Alberta's Local Governments and Their Politics.* Edmonton: University of Alberta Press, 1985.

Metis Association of Alberta and Joe Sawchuk, Patricia Sawchuk and Theresa Ferguson. *Metis Land Rights in Alberta: A Political History.* Edmonton: Metis Association of Alberta, 1981.

Morton, W.L. *Manitoba, A History.* 2nd ed. Toronto: University of Toronto Press, 1967.

Peterson, Jacqueline and Jennifer S.H. Brown. *The New Peoples: Being and Becoming Metis in North America.* Winnipeg: University of Manitoba Press, 1985.

Pitkin, Hannah F. *The Concept of Representation.* Berkeley: University of California Press, 1972.

Purich, Donald. *Our Land: Native Rights in Canada.* Toronto: James Lorimer & Company, 1986.

Purich, Donald. *The Metis.* Toronto: James Lorimer & Company, 1988.

Redbird, Duke. *We Are Metis, A Metis View of the Development of a Native Canadian People.* Willowdale: Ontario Metis & Non Status Indian Association, 1980.

Sealey, D. Bruce and Antoine S. Lussier, eds. *The Metis: Canada's Forgotten People.* Winnipeg: Pemmican Publications, 1975.

Shkilnyk, Anastasia M. *A Poison Stronger Than Love: The Destruction of an Ojibwa Community.* New Haven: Yale University Press, 1985.

Stanley, George F.G. *The Birth of Western Canada: A History of the Riel Rebellions*. 1936. Reprint, Toronto: University of Toronto Press, 1960.

Sprague, D.N. and R.P. Frye. *The Genealogy of the First Metis Nation*. Winnipeg: Pemmican Publications, 1983.

Publications of the Alberta Federation of Metis Settlements

"By Means of Conferences and Associations" We Ensure Our Rights. 1986.

Council Handbook. N.d. (updated periodically).

East Prairie Metis, 1939-1979: 40 Years of Determination. N.d.

Elizabeth Metis Settlement: A Local History. Nd.

Metisism: A Canadian Identity. 1982.

Our Home: A History of Kikino Metis Settlement. 1984.

Publications of the Government of Alberta

Alberta's Metis Settlements: A Compendium of Background Documents. (Native Secretariat) 1984.

Implementation of Resolution 18. (Municipal Affairs) 1982.

Report of the MacEwan Joint Metis-Government Committee to Review the Metis Betterment Act and Regulations. (Municipal Affairs) 1984.

Report of the Royal Commission on the Condition of the Halfbreed Population of the Province of Alberta [The Ewing Commission]. 1936.

Other

Hill, Judith. "The Ewing Commission, 1935: A Case Study in Metis-Government Relations." Unpublished honours essay, University of Alberta, 1977.

INDEX

A
Adams, Howard, 21
Alberta Act, 63, 142, 143, 146, 147, 151
Alberta Federation of Metis Settlement Associations. *See* Federation of Metis Settlement Associations
Asch, Michael, 135
Assimilation, 18

B
Battle of Seven Oaks, 3
Big Prairie Metis Settlement, 27
Boldt, Menno, 135
Brady, James, 10, 14, 15
Braithwaite, E.A., 12
Braybrooke, David, 135
Brown, Jennifer S.H., 21
Brownlee, Premier J.E., 11
Buffalo Lake Metis Settlement, 27
"*By Means of Conferences and Negotiations*," 144-46, 147, 152

C
Cardinal, Harold, ix
Caslan Metis Settlement, 27
Cold Lake Metis Settlement, 27
Commission agreement, 151-52
Concerned Citizens, 150
Constitution Act, 7, 61
Cumming, Peter A., 22

D
Dahl, Robert A., 121
Davies, Percy, 11
Dechene, Joseph, 10
Dene Declaration, 135
Department of Lands and Mines (Alberta), 10, 11, 16
Department of Municipal Affairs (Alberta), xiv, 35, 37, 80, 81; assistant deputy minister for Improvements Districts, 38, 66, 74, 144; minister, 37; Native Services Unit, 74
Department of Public Welfare (Alberta), 30
Department of the Attorney General (Alberta), 80, 147, 149
Dion, Joseph, 10, 14
Dobbin, Murray, 22
Dosman, Edgar, ix
Douglas, J.M., 12
Driben, Paul, 22
Duggan, D.M., 11
Dumont, Gabriel, 4

E

East Prairie Metis Settlement, 27
Elders, 57-59
Elders committees, 145
Elizabeth Metis Settlement, 27
Ewing, A.F., 12, 14-15
Ewing Commission, 12-21; Report of, 15-21
Equality before the law, 125, 126

F

Favouritism, 83, 107-8, 115-19, 130, 133, 148
Federation of Metis Settlement Associations, x, xi, xiii, 38, 111, 112, 121, 137, 138, 144, 145, 147, 148, 151; and the Metis Association of Alberta, 40; assessment of by settlement councillors, 70-71; board of directors of, 64-69; executive council of, 64-65; president of, 39, 144, 149, 151; Task Force on Resolution 18, 144

G

Getty, Premier Don, 145, 149, 151
Gift Lake Metis Settlement, 27
Giraud, Marcel, 21
Grant, Cuthbert, 4
Great Depression, xiii, 5, 9, 12, 21, 139

H

Hill, Judith, 22
Howard, Joseph K., 21
Hudson's Bay Company, 3, 4

I

Indian treaties, 6, 7
Inuit, 7
Implementation of Resolution 18, 147-49

J

Johnston, J. Paul, 136

K

Kikino Metis Settlement, 27

L

Lacombe, Father Albert, 7, 8
"Leading families," 92, 116-118
Long, J. Anthony, 135
Lougheed, Premier Peter E., 64, 138, 142, 143
Lussier, Antoine S., 21, 22

M

MacEwan, Grant, 62, 71
MacEwan Committee (MacEwan Joint Metis-Government Committee), 62-63, 71, 138, 141, 143; Report of, 141, 143, 152
"Made in Alberta" approach, 63, 142-52
Manitoba Act, 4
Masson, Jack, 121

Metis: definition of, by Ewing Commission, 17; definition of, in Metis Population Betterment Act, 25; definition of, in Report of MacEwan Committee, 142
Metis arbitration tribunals, 145
Metis Association of Alberta, 9, 10-12, 39-40, 101-2, 142, 150, 153-54
Metis Betterment Act, 24-26, 31, 32, 33, 40, 41, 62-63, 137
Metis Coalition Society of Alberta, 148, 150
Metis culture, 80, 104, 131, 140, 141
Metis Development Branch, xii, xiv, 66, 74, 100, 107, 111-12; assessment of, by settlement councillors, 79-82; director of, 74, 144; district offices, 74, 75, 82; finances of, 75-79; organization of, 63-64; seizure of documents from settlements by, 62, 138; staff of, 74-75; views of Metis settlements, 82-84
Metisism: A Canadian Identity, 138-41, 152
Metis National Council, 40
Metis Population Betterment Act, 21, 24-25, 29
Metis Population Trust Account: establishment of, 34; legal provisions regarding, 34; litigation concerning, 34, 137
Metis Rehabilitation Branch, 30, 73
Metis settlement associations, 25, 26; general meetings of, 41; provisions governing membership in, 29, 41, 142-43, 150
Metis settlements: allotment of land within, 28-29; constitutions, 29-32; finances, 32-34; subsurface rights on, 34
Metis Settlements Act, 146-48, 151
Metis Settlements General Council, 148, 152
Metis Settlements Land Act, 151
Metis Settlements Resources Trust Fund, 146
Metis settlers. *See* Settlers
Mickenberg, Neil H., 22
Moore, Marvin E., 71
Morgan, Kenneth, 22

N

Native Secretariat (Alberta), xii
Nicks, Trudy, 22
Norris, Malcolm, 10, 13, 14
North-West Rebellion, 1, 4, 21

O

Okimawiwin, 145-46, 148
Ombudsman (Alberta), 62, 138
Orr, Dr. Harold, 14

P

Paddle Prairie Metis Settlement, 27
Peterson, Jacqueline, 2, 21
Pitkin, Hannah F., 136
Plain, Fred, 135
Pocklington, T.C., 136
Political health, 103, 119-21, 128, 133
Political self-determination, 87, 88, 103, 120, 123-35, 143, 153; degrees of, 123; legal approach to, 124-25; rights-based approach to, 125-27; well-being approach to, 127; well-being approach to, applied to Alberta Metis settlements, 127-34
Purich, Donald, 21

R

Redbird, Duke, 3, 21, 22
Red River Settlement, 1, 3
Red River uprising, 4
Reid, R.G., 11
Resolution 18, 143-44, 149
Riel, Louis, 1, 4-5
Royal Canadian Mounted Police, 43, 50-51, 97-98, 133-34

S

St. Paul des Metis, 7-9, 12, 14
Sawchuk, Joe, 22
Sawchuk, Patricia, 22
Scott, Thomas, 5
Scrip, 6, 16
Sealey, Bruce, 21, 22
Self-government. *See* Political self-determination
Settlement councillors: attitudes towards police, 50-51; opinions about local issues, 56-60; opinions about political role of elders, 57-59; opinions about political self-determination, 59-60; orientations towards the Metis Association of Alberta, 52-53; views about federal officials, 49-50; views about provincial officials, 52; voting in federal elections, 49-50; voting in provincial elections, 51-52
Settlement councils: chairmen of, 30, 36, 43-44; election of, 36; eligibility to serve on, 29-30; general powers of, 36-40, 148; informal powers of, 42-43; ordinary meetings of, 30; relationships with Federation of Metis Settlements, 38; relationships with Metis Association of Alberta, 39-40; social composition of, 46-49; special meetings of, 30; specific powers of, 40-42
Settlement Sooniyaw, 39
Settlers: demographic characteristics of, 91-95; evaluations of settlement councils, 105-9; opinions about local problems, 109-10; opinions about political self-determination, 110-14; orientations to the Federation of Metis Settlement Associations, 113-15; orientations to the Metis Association of Alberta, 101-2; views about favouritism, 115-19; voting in federal elections, 96-98; voting in provincial elections, 98-101; voting in settlement elections, 105-6
Slattery, Brian, 135
Social Credit Party, 12, 21
Stanley, George F.G., 2, 21, 22
Sprague, D.N., 21
Spry, Irene M., 22

T

Therien, Father Adeodat, 8

U

United Farmers of Alberta, 9, 11, 21

V

Voting. *See* Federation of Metis Settlement Associations, settlement councillors, settlers

W

Westlock Resolution, 142-43, 144, 145
Wolf Lake Metis Settlement, 27

Pat-439-2410